Copyright © 2013 James A. Nelson
All rights reserved.

ISBN: 1484947967
ISBN 13: 9781484947968
Library of Congress Control Number: 2013909223
CreateSpace Independent Publishing Platform
North Charleston, South Carolina

ROCK HILL

James A. Nelson

BUDDY NELSON'S HANGAR *is as big as man's imagination. There are no locks on the doors and the only membership requirements are Curiosity, Faith, Desire and Determination.*

INTRODUCTION

This story is a work of *faction*: make-believe with a few facts. I have always thought this to be true of most fiction we read. I suspect that is why some Literature is so believable and lasting: either someone actually lived the life or could have.

The only real people in this tale are Jim: Jupe and Daisy (my dad and mom); my Aunt Agnes: my Uncles Alvin, Cliff, Earl, and Sandy; my Grandpa and Grandma; my cousin Harold; Joe Kirkwood; Rocky Marciano; Harlem Globetrotter Coach Mr. Elmer H. Ripley and Harlem Globetrotter Star Mr. "Goose" Tatum, and Mr. Molt Taylor, Creator of the Aerocar.

I would like to thank my classmates of over sixty years ago for sharing a part of their lives with me. Through the years, I have thought fondly of those days many times.

If anything in this story helps one person get through a difficult day, the work involved in creating this book will have been worthwhile.

DEDICATION

This book is dedicated to my wife, Marylil, who has been willing to tolerate my sense of humor and other shortcomings for forty seven years. I would also like to honor my four children and one grandson who in their own ways are creating successful careers. Marylil and I are happy they have exciting and interesting lives: Sabryna Apollo Bach (Writer and Business Owner); US Army WO3 Darrick James Martin Nelson (Chinook Helicopter Instructor Pilot); Vanessa Angelica Nelson-McCalister (Insurance Agent and Equestrian Horse Rider/Owner); Tyrone Forrest Nelson (Massage Therapist and Aesthetician): and grandson US Army PFC Tyler Darrick Nelson is seeking a future filled with great experiences and outstanding opportunities, starting with the U.S. Army.

ACKNOWLEDGMENTS

I would like to acknowledge a few special people who were instrumental in the creation of this book. **FIRST:** My wife, Marylil, who started out as "Clerk Typist," then promoted herself first to "Editor" and finally to "Writer" as the copy returned totally changed from what I thought I had written. She said "Oh, but I believe my changes read a little better." **SECOND**: my daughter Vanessa Nelson-McCalister who saved *Rock Hill* on her computer until I finally decided to finish this work. **THIRD:** Ms. Cathy Pedigo from the State of Kentucky, a gorgeous woman who is a whiz on the keyboard and extremely intelligent as well. **FOURTH:** my son Tyrone Nelson who with his professional computer skills e-mailed the manuscript in a Word document to the Editor and helped his parents with the IT challenges.

I would also like to thank my "LISTENERS" - - those respected Loved Ones, Dear Friends, and Esteemed Associates who listened to some of what I had written. The listing of their names does not mean any or all agreed with my writing: Ms. Sabryna Bach, Ms. Judy Bailey, Mr. Albert E. Carter, Ms. Tonya Chapman, Mr. Ed Denmon, Captain Marty Fedigan, Mr. and Mrs. Fred Gershick, Dr. George Ghosn, Mr. Sanford J. Grasseth, Ms. Christine Hassing, Ms. Betty Hess, Mr. Jim Honke, Mr. Charles F. Jackson, Ms. Patricia Johnson, Mr. Samy Khoury, Mrs. Vanessa Nelson-McCalister, Mrs. Vivian Mohns, Mr. Darrick Nelson, Mrs. Marylil Nelson, Mr. Tyrone Nelson, Mr. Robert Nordlie, Mr. Kevin O'Brien, Mrs. Cathy Pedigo, Mr. Howard L. Phillips, Attorney at Law, Mrs. Louise Pruitt, Mr. Ben P. R. Roose, Ms. Mary Jo Sato, Ms. Sherry Stance, Mr. Dick Stiles, Ms. Laura Walter, Ms. Catherine Waters, Mr. Jerry Weible, Mr. Brad Wollen and Mr. James M. Womack, Attorney at Law.

SPECIAL NOTE

The humor in this story may offend some; for that I apologize in advance. A long time ago, I had a very wonderful Teacher wise beyond my years who said, "Jim, you have a special gift that God gave you - a precious sense of humor that is infectious and original. I pray you never lose that gift, especially when life gets tough and people or places are cruel. I believe you have been placed on this earth to help yourself by helping others. Sometimes that help may be in the form of making others laugh to help them through the ordeals of life. In our busy life, which we often think is so all-important and absolutely necessary, fate occasionally throws us insurmountable obstacles that break our hearts. This is when your sense of humor will be a godsend to enable you and others to survive and excel."

Capitalization of certain words may offend the more gifted in the written word. My Editor, Ms. Bessie of Create Space, did a great job of informing me about the *Chicago Manuel of Style*. My wife Marylil Vivian, my daughter Sabryna Apollo and my son Darrick James Martin agreed with this "Lady of Very Esteemed Erudition". However, this Author reserved the right to honor the status of Certain People or "Things" with a capital letter! So There! Get over it! In My Opinion, There Is Not Enough Courtesy And Respect For Others In Our World Today.

Remember what President Lincoln said a long time ago when he was criticized for telling jokes as the future of the United States of America hung in the balance on the battlefield:

"If I did not laugh, I should die!"

TABLE OF CONTENTS

ELEMENTARY SCHOOL 1

JUNIOR HIGH 73

They don't grow them like this any more!.

ELEMENTARY SCHOOL

The year is 1949. My name is Jim, I am eleven years old. I am in Miss Charlotte Heart's fifth grade class at Rock Hill Elementary School. I live in a small logging and sawmill community named Rock Hill in southwest Washington State. I am an only child now. But Mom is pregnant. My Dad is a professional logger with his own company in partnership with two brothers-in-law: World War II Veterans Uncle Sandy and Uncle Alvin. Dad says our Country is enjoying an economic boom after years of suffering and doing without while we were fighting the Japanese and Germans to win World War II.

The loggers are working six and seven days a week to supply the sawmills with timber to cut into lumber to build new homes throughout America for our U.S. Military Veterans and their families. Plus, practically every mountain top around

Rock Hill

Rock Hill has a railroad tie mill running full bore. That's because the US Government has authorized funds to help the railroad companies rebuild the railroad track beds across America that were destroyed by heavy use during World War II.

Jobs are plentiful; workers are hard to find. People are making more money than ever. It is an economic miracle. Dad and Mom both say now that there is true peace on earth that our prosperous life should last a long, long time. It is a great time to be an American, a citizen of the greatest, most powerful, most generous country on this earth. Everyone on earth wants to be an American, or act like one!

My favorite Teacher, Miss Charlotte Heart, told my Parents that I have a curious mind, a determination to succeed, and a wonderful sense of humor. She also maintains I talk too much in class. When corrected, I am quiet - for a while. Miss Heart says, "Sometimes less is more." Because Miss Heart is a very smart woman and a wonderful Teacher, I try my best to watch my tongue. However, my strong feelings and ideas at times outweigh my ability to remain quiet. My Dad and Mom say that in addition to always living my life based upon honesty and integrity, I should be more watchful about my conduct in the classroom. I told them that even if I talk too much, I always say things I truly believe. For example: Like Dad, when Mom has her baby, I want it to be a boy!

There is absolutely no doubt about it. The only thing I want is a brother. A guy I can teach the things that I already know. Things like how to skip rocks across the water and how to catch frogs in the heat of the day and how tell the difference between a P- 40 and a P-51. Why, I'd protect him, too. Say if he got to spitting at kids and calling them names, why, I'd tell him to stop and I'd tell the other kids to let him alone. I'd be quick about it too. He and I'd do almost everything together. We'd play baseball and Indian Wrestle and fish and fly airplanes together. Everything! There is nothing we wouldn't do.

Why, I don't know what I'd do if Mom had a girl. Just take this simple question: What could I ever do with a sister? Nothing, that's what. You can't teach a girl anything that a boy would want to know. You can't even go number one off the bridge together. How about at night? You wouldn't think of running away from home to pull "The Gunny Sack Trick" with your sister of all people, would you? You don't know what "The Gunny Sack Trick" is, do you? I better tell you, because - it's really something! What The Gang plans to do is get a regular gunny sack and fill it full of rags and paper to make it look like a body. We plan to tie a rope about thirty feet long at the top of the sack to make a head and give us something to jerk the sack with; then we'll put the sack on the highway where a driver can't miss seeing it.

Boy, it'll sure be something to see a car slow down because the driver thinks it's a real body lying in the road. Once the car has stopped in front of the sack, we'll all pull on the rope as hard as we can. People will sure act differently when the sack takes off! I bet sometimes they will just honk their horn; other times they will get out of their cars and shout dirty words at us. Of course, we won't hang around to listen. After the sack is jerked, we'll take off just like we do when school is over for the day.

We can't do it very often though. If we did, the police might lock us up forever if we get caught. Anyway, a girl wouldn't have the good sense to jerk the rope at the right time. Neither would she keep her trap shut when folks started asking questions about strange things seen out on the highway. That's for sure!

Nope, a girl just wouldn't fit in. Take this summer. There you'd be, she'd go off to some Rock Hill Church Camp somewhere and you'd be left alone shagging foul balls all by yourself. Oh, she'd write all right. But what good is that? Who in the world wants to read what Sally, Jane, and Mary and all the rest of those silly girlfriends of hers are doing? Why, there ain't a guy alive who would give his worst pury marble or a chipped steely, for that matter, to find out: I mean, just who in the world wants to know something like that anyway?

Now, shagging foul balls. I'll bet that doesn't sound like much to you, does it? Well it is. In fact, one day I made a whole dollar doing just that. Oh I would have done it for nothing as far as that goes. But I mean the Rock Hill Outlaws paid me to do it. And racking bats. There is not a girl in the world who knows how to rack bats right. I'll bet they'd have 'em crossed in no time. You know what that means. Why, if a guy goes up with a bat that's been crossed, he might as well not even go to the plate. He wouldn't even have a chance. He'd strike out for sure. The pitcher would fog it by the batter so fast he wouldn't even know when the ball flew by. You can bet on that!

Of course I really didn't want to take the money. It's an honor to shagg foul balls and rack the bats. Our team, the Rock Hill Outlaws, is a semipro team sponsored by a local sawmill. Mr. Fred Hester, the Rock Hills Barber, is the Manager, and it was his decision to hire me. He said that he really likes my enthusiasm and energy. He says my attitude could really help "sparkplug" the Outlaws. Now, I only shagg foul balls and rack the bats for all the games at home. Mom won't let me travel with the Outlaws. She says I am too young to be going with strangers so far away from home. Of course I'm mad about it and think she's nuts, but Mom won't budge from her decision. My Dad says it's up to my Mom, and she told him in no uncertain words: "You bet it is, and don't you ever forget it!" Dad just laughed and winked at me.

The Outlaws have some really good local guys: "Beef" Harrison plays a fantastic third base and can hit a ball out of the park; Tommy Foster, the catcher, can throw a guy out trying to steal second while sitting on his haunches; and Lefty Shell, the Rock Hill High School Baseball Coach, plays first base and occasionally pitches. Tommy Foster says Lefty throws a pretty mean curve, which many batters say is major league quality, but the only problem with Lefty is he can also be wilder than a garbage dump tom cat.

Plus, The Outlaws have a few outstanding players from other places who were hired to first play baseball and second to work part time at the sawmill during baseball season. A number of these fellows have actually played professionally. Some have even climbed as high as Triple - A ball. Matt Wilson is a guy from Alabama who pitches for us. "Beef" told me Matt once struck out Babe Ruth in an exhibition game. During practice I asked Matt about it, and he said, "Yeah, it's true, but in the same game the Babe also hit two home runs off me. The second one hit a coon sitting in a tree out beyond the left-field fence." The players and I all laughed.

When I told my Mom the story later, she slapped my face hard! I couldn't believe it. I must have looked bewildered because she said, "Listen, young man, the word 'coon' is a nasty word that only ignorant people use when talking about Black people, and using that kind of language shows a lack of respect and courtesy toward others."

Mom said, "When I was a little girl growing up in the Ozarks, I had a number of Black friends." To her they were all good people, and she hated how some White people mistreated Black people. She said, "You should always judge people by the goodness of their heart, the brains in their head, and their willingness to help others less fortunate."

My Dad added, "Yes, and the sweat off their brow doesn't hurt either."

Mom said, "You are lucky to be born with White skin in a world where some people are not color-blind." She said, "Many Black people have been mistreated throughout their lives by some idiots who think they are better than others just because of their White skin."

ELEMENTARY SCHOOL

Boy, was I sorry. I thought Matt Wilson had been talking about a real raccoon in a tree! I'd never want to hurt someone's feelings about their race or color, that's for sure. But Mom slapping me so hard was sure a surprise! It brought back a memory that I had almost forgotten. It was something that happened when I was six or seven years old.

One cold winter Sunday morning Mom had fixed fried eggs, sausage, potatoes, and hotcakes for breakfast. Boy, I liked hotcakes, but Mom seldom fixed them; she always said waffles were easier to make. I had eaten one hotcake, and when I asked for more, I hollered out, "Pass the hotcocks, please!" Boy, did my Mother slap me! It knocked me clean off the stool I was sitting on! Funny thing is, I didn't even realize I had said a bad word. At my age I truly didn't know the difference between a *cock* and a *cake*. I just knew the word sounded kind of funny. But, boy, my Mom sure did! I swore to myself as I was rubbing my jaw that one day I too would find out what the bad word meant that I had used. Murderin' Sam and The Gang got a real laugh when I told them the story. They all said I was lucky to live through that experience. You know, I can never eat hotcakes without thinking about that Sunday morning. It's funny how a little old rap on the head will leave a long memory.

The Rock Hill Outlaws play town teams from nearby Morton, Toledo, Longview, Centralia, and Aberdeen. We play in the Tri-County League. At the end of the summer, the league champion goes to Tacoma to play in the regional league tournament with the winner going to Nationals in Wichita,

Kansas. The Outlaws have never won the league championship, but they try awfully hard and have come close a time or two. The townspeople are really proud of them.

The baseball games are a big event in Rock Hill. They are played on Saturday and Sunday afternoons with nearly the whole town in attendance. This is as close to professional baseball as most Rock Hill fans ever get. All of the Major League Baseball teams are back East, and few local people have much of an opportunity to even see the Portland Beavers or the Seattle Rainiers in the Pacific Coast League. Only Mr. Malley Damer, who owns Damer's Hardware Store and drives to Seattle quite often for supplies, gets to see the Seattle Rainiers on a regular basis. Mr. Damer always talks about watching Jungle Jim Ravera play for the Rainiers. He says he knew Jungle Jim was a surefire major league prospect. Mr. Damer was proven right when Jungle Jim was called up to the major leagues by the Chicago White Sox.

Once, on a trip to Illinois for a hardware convention, he saw the New York Yankees play the Chicago White Sox. He couldn't wait to get home to Rock Hill to tell everyone about seeing Mickey Mantle throw out Jungle Jim trying to score from third base after Mickey caught a fly in deep center field. Mickey must have quite an arm because Jungle Jim is one fast base runner.

One game I will never forget is when the Rock Hill Outlaws played the Jackson Street Sluggers of Seattle. Boy, was that something! The Sluggers were loaded with talent and featured a few guys who had played on a couple of National

Negro League teams back East before the War. This particular game was a Sunday afternoon feature of the Rock Hills Pioneer Days Celebration, a summer event to recognize leading members of the community and bring visitors to town to spend money at the restaurants, gas stations, and grocery stores.

Saturday morning always features a parade of floats by the garden club, the Lion's Club, local businesses, the Rock Hill High School girls running for Pioneer Days Queen, and some floats from other towns advertising their own summer festivals. The Rock Hill High School Band also marches and plays in the parade. They look super in their colorful red and black uniforms and sound fantastic. Saturday afternoon usually features a Junior Legion baseball game between Rock Hill and nearby Onalaska. Saturday night is filled with a live music program in the High School gym by local country music bands. The Pioneer Days Queen is crowned during the middle of the performance. The winner is based on which girl has sold the most Pioneer Days badges. All of the girls look beautiful in their formals. Dad once said, "Men always like to buy things from and for pretty girls." Then he winked at my Mom!

A carnival from Arizona comes to town on Thursday and opens Friday and Saturday at eleven a.m. running until midnight. Sunday it opens at noon and closes at six p.m. Some of the older boys are hired to help set up and take down the rides and tents. I really like the Ferris Wheel, the Merry-Go-Round, and the Rotating Swing that flies high in the air. There are also plenty of games of chance where it's possible to win stuffed

Rock Hill

animals and trinkets. I like the games where you throw baseballs at steel milk bottles. I've also thrown rings around the necks of pop bottles too, but I was not very good at that game.

The Jackson Street Sluggers were leading the Seattle Metro Semipro League when they came to Rock Hill to play a baseball game on Sunday afternoon of Pioneer Days. By their swagger and attitude you could tell the Sluggers had great pride and knew they were very good. They thought a trip to Rock Hill would lead to an easy victory. But were the Sluggers in for a surprise! First, the Rock Hill Outlaws are a very good baseball team. Second, the Sluggers hadn't counted on Homer Wren, Our Resident Umpire!

It was the top of the ninth inning; the score was four to three in favor of the Outlaws. The Sluggers were up. Two outs, bases loaded with the Sluggers cleanup hitter at bat. The first pitch was low and just a cat hair outside. The pitch could have been called either way. The batter chose not to swing.

"Strike one." Umpire Homer called.

The second pitch, the Slugger clean up hitter hit clear over the barbed wire fence in left field, just foul: A gigantic, towering three hundred and fifty foot smasher !

"Strike two."

The third pitch was in the dirt, blocked by catcher Tommy.
"Ball one."

The count was two strikes, one ball, two outs. The fourth and final pitch of the game was high and inside. The batter chose not to swing once again. The ball could have been called either way.

ELEMENTARY SCHOOL

"Strike three." said Umpire Homer Wren.

Three outs! Game over! Outlaws win!

Pandemonium broke loose. The Sluggers all came running out of their dugout, complaining they had been robbed! They were just out of luck. The game was in the books! For his protection, Umpire Homer Wren was escorted off the field by Rock Hill's Police Chief Earl Horton, and Lewis County Deputy Sheriff Bill Lawson.

Earlier in the game, the cleanup hitter had hit a home run over the barbed wire fence in centerfield. After the game, Mr. Hester and a couple of players measured the distance. It was over 410 feet in length.

Matt Wilson said their cleanup batter was from Atlanta, Georgia, and was well known throughout the South as one of baseball's finest hitters. Both the cleanup batter and the catcher had earlier in their careers been stars in the National Negro League. The Slugger's catcher had caught games pitched by Satchel Paige many times. Mr. Hester said that both ball players could have played in either The American or The National Baseball Leagues, if Blacks had been permitted to play. Matt also said the only other man he ever saw hit a ball that far was the Babe. In fact, Matt said he once saw Babe Ruth when he was over forty years old hit a ball over 450 feet in length, clear out of a ballpark stadium. Matt laughed when he said that Babe thought he could hit home runs until he was seventy years old - if the league would let someone else run the bases for him!

Rock Hill

The next week when I went into Mr. Hester's Barbershop for a haircut, I asked Mr. Hester about the way the Sluggers game had ended. He said, "Well, Jim, you witnessed one of life's lessons on the baseball diamond. In the ninth inning when a visiting team like the Sluggers is behind in the score and up to bat with two outs, the batter better swing at every pitch that's either in or close to the strike zone. The hometown umpire, more often than not, is going to give the benefit of the size of the strike zone to the hometown pitcher.

"It's not cheating. It's not robbing a team of a victory. It's just baseball as played in real life. Now, I'm not talking about taking a game away from another team that has won the game hands down. I'm talking about a game so close the winner is a genuine toss-up. Such was the game between the Sluggers and the Outlaws.

"The first mistake the Slugger team made was coming to Rock Hill thinking the Outlaws represented an automatic easy victory. **That is a good lesson for you, Jim: Never Underestimate Your Opponent.** Second, the Slugger cleanup hitter made a terrible error in not swinging at either one of those close pitches that could have been called either a strike or a ball. With his batting power and skill, the man could have just as easily won the game with a grand slam home run. We'll never know because the batter didn't even try. **That is another good lesson for you, Jim: In life, be aggressive. Be smart at the same time, but DO NOT sit back waiting for someone else to take action.**

"It's an old adage in baseball that you have to swing the bat to hit the ball. The teams who swing the bat the most and the best usually win the most games. The umpire rarely has much of an impact on who actually wins or loses. Usually the toughest part of his job is to rule on base-running disputes to keep the game rolling along. Most pitches are fairly easy to call correctly."

The Rock Hill Outlaws also have a basketball team in the wintertime. Mr. Hester asked me to be the ball boy for home games. He said my work on the baseball field had proven him right about my energy and desire to win. He said he was very proud of me. Boy, it made me feel terrific!

Once again, Rock Hill has a great team. The Rock Hill High School Basketball Coach, Scooter Davis, plays guard just like a pro. He passes the ball behind his back and is an unbelievable dribbler. In College in Oklahoma, Scooter had been such a good player he was asked to play for the US Olympic team. The Getzler brothers, Ralph and George, play guard and forward and are terrific shooters as well as great at rebounding. "Beef" Harrison plays both center and forward and is awfully rugged on defense. To round out the first five players on the team are the Parker brothers, Ted and Bob. They take turns playing forward with the Getzler brothers. I especially like Bob, who flew a Boeing B-17 bomber in the European Theater during World War II. Bob is awfully quiet and never talks about his experiences. Mr. Hester told me Bob flew some awfully dangerous missions and considers him- self very lucky to have lived through the ordeal of enemy flak bursts in the skies over Germany.

My Dad told me that many of the US Military Veterans of World War II who actually experienced the most dangerous action seldom talk about their combat. Having had to endure the trauma once was enough. "Just for entertainment," Dad said, "to ask any Veteran to relive moments of pure, cold fear when a man's courage is tested is cruel. **These are two good lessons, Jim: ONE, Mind your own business. TWO, do not be a braggart. Actions alone will always speak volumes.**"

Our traditional basketball rival is from Morton . Boy, are they good! Our games against Morton are always standing room only. Morton has a seven-foot center by the name of Big Bill Big, the local Washington State Game Warden. I got to know Mr. Big, and he is a very friendly guy—funny thing, I have always noticed most big guys are usually the gentlest people.

The games are always very close, with Morton usually winning, unfortunately, by a point or two. Morton's basketball team is a sight to behold. In addition to Mr. Big Bill Big, the seven-foot center, Morton has a guard who started for the University of Washington varsity team, Mr. Wily Low. He is over six feet and is smooth as spider silk in passing and handling the ball. Scooter Davis says Willy is as fine a guard as he has ever played against - That is saying a lot because when Scooter was playing in the Olympics, he played with and against some of the best basketball players in the world. The Burgy brothers, Mike and Paul, play forward and are absolute demons on the backboards. They rarely miss a rebound and shoot pretty well, too. Finally, the Morton High School Basketball Coach, Gil Shannon, plays the other guard. Gil is known for racking up a lot of points by stealing the ball from his opponents in every game. He is lightning quick with his hands and feet, too!

One of my favorite players on Rock Hill's team is Marion Johnson, a very friendly good-sized guy who plays forward for us but actually lives in Centralia. Marion delivers bread to the grocery stores in Rock Hill and knows a lot of people in town. He played football at Washington State College the year the Cougars played in the Rose Bowl; then he went on to a career with the Washington Redskins in the National Football League. Marion also has a really movie-star beautiful wife named Dixie who is very nice to me and is always telling me that I do a very good job as the ball boy. Dixie also says I am a very handsome guy and it is a good thing for Marion that she met him before she met me. Marion just laughs, and I say she is just being nice and I do not believe a word of it!

By the way, a famous story about Mr. Big Bill Big occurred some years ago when he was boxing professionally. He trained in Tacoma and set his sights on the heavyweight championship title. Before retiring, he had won a number of bouts and at one time had been ranked number two or three by *Ring Magazine*. He even boxed a time or two at Madison Square Gardens in New York City.

Once in response to an ad for sparring partners, a Ft. Lewis Army Private by the name of Rocky Marciano crawled into the ring with Big Bill Big. The practice bout was rated a draw. Later, when Rocky was the Heavyweight Champion Of The World, in response to a New York sports writer's question about any unusual opponents, Rocky recalled the time when he tried to hit a seven-foot giant with arms the size of Douglas Fir tree trunks. By the way he plays basketball, anyone can see Mr. Big Bill Big is truly a great athlete. You should see the size of his hands. Wow, are they huge! When Big Bill holds a basketball, it practically disappears. It looks like it's the size of a softball in his hands.

When the name of The Heavyweight Champion Of The World, Mr. Rocky Marciano, comes up, I always think of another famous boxer who is a full-fledged Hollywood movie star: Mr. Joe Kirkwood, the man who plays the character Joe Palooka in the Joe Palooka movies that occasionally play at the Z Theater in Rock Hill on Tuesday and Wednesday nights. The Gang really likes Joe Palooka, and we never miss his movies.

While I was listening one afternoon to a sports radio interview program from radio station KELA in Centralia, an interviewer asked Mr. Kirkwood about his boxing experiences. "In preparing for your Joe Palooka movies," the interviewer asked, "did you ever box any professional boxers we might know?"

Mr. Kirkwood said, "How about Rocky Marciano? Is he good enough for you?"

The interviewer replied, "Yes! What was it like? How did you do?"

Mr. Kirkwood said, "Well, it was like being hit by two twenty-five-pound sledgehammers at the same time over and over. Rocky's punches were devastating! That man can hit so hard it is unbelievable. He aimed for my upper body. After a blast of punches, my arms and shoulders began to hurt like the worst toothache I ever had. Pretty soon, it was impossible for me to lift my arms to throw a punch back. Then, the boxing match was all over. Rocky had me. How did I do? I lost. But I did win the knowledge of just how strong and good The Heavyweight Champion Of The World, Mr. Rocky Marciano, really is!"

⌘ ⌘ ⌘

To tell you the truth, I just know Mom wants a baby girl. Let me ask you who in his right mind would want to have a girl in The Gang? Who, I ask you? Why, I'd be the laughing stock of The Gang. I can just see me walking up to Murderin' Sam or Tiger Terry or Sleepy John, for that matter, and telling - 'em I wanted to get my sister in The Gang. I can just see how far I'd get. Why, they'd tell me to go to you-know-where and never come back. I wouldn't, either. You can be darn sure of that! You can't blame them. For instance, how would you ask a girl to pull her shirt up and take the Black Scar across her stomach? I can just see it. At first she'd giggle. There is not a girl alive that doesn't giggle. Everybody knows that when you take the Black Scar it's no laughing matter. It's like going to Church or a funeral even. Everybody knows you are not supposed to laugh at a place like that. When it came time to put the burnt stick across her stomach, she'd start lookin' kinda scaredy cattish. Pretty soon, she'd start crying. Oh that would really take the cake. I can just see Murderin' Sam watching my sister shedding real tears. He would give me a look that said:

"I Told You So If You Had Any Brains You Would be Dangerous"

And, who knows, they might even kick me out of The Gang!

Another thing. How're you gonna expect a girl to lie on her back and let her Mosquito Blood Brothers walk across her chest frontward and backward or let us do a switch-leg-jump-step right over the top of her head? (You can't close your eyes either. If you do, you're out—no questions asked.) Take the simple thing of allowing a mosquito to land on your arm and then bite you. When you think he's sucked enough blood, you hit him from at least thirteen inches away. Then you smear his body and your blood into the sign of an X on your arm. Now I ask you: do you think there's a girl alive that could stand to do that? No, there is not, and you know it! For sure, she would just think it was a stupid thing to do.

Sometimes I think that if Mom has a girl, I'll run away from home. I wouldn't tell anyone. I'd just up and do it in the black of night. I mean, I know what would happen if Mom had a girl. Pretty soon it would be "Son, would please you do this?" and "Son, would you please do that?" And CaZooks, before I could say the Mosquito Blood Brothers Password,

ELEMENTARY SCHOOL

Mom would have me taking care of my sister full time! I bet you'd never guess what the Password is. Never in a thousand years! If you really want to know, it is: "Blue Bird Cow Pile Sassa Frass Tea." Neat, isn't it? You have to say it real fast, too. If you don't say it real fast, they'd never let down the rope to our tree house. Also, before you say the Password, you must look all six directions—frontward, backward, sideward, sideward, upward, and downward—to make sure there are no Kraut or Jap spies listening.

First, Mom would send me for something simple like a towel. Then it would be warming bottles. You know what would be next? YIP! I'll tell you. I'd be changing diapers! I almost can't bear to think of it. I'd have to handle all those dirty, stinky, smelly diapers! Why, I'd have to learn how to do it real fast because I wouldn't dare take a breath. Who knows, if I ran into trouble like losing a safety pin, and it took longer than usual, I might suffocate even.

And The Gang! What do you think would happen if they found out I was changing diapers? What do you think they would do? I'll tell you what they would do. They'd die right where they were standing when whoever squealed on me told them. I mean, they really would too. They'd laugh so hard and they'd probably never get over it. When they saw me, that's when I'd die. Course I wouldn't let 'em see me. I couldn't afford to. I'd probably just have to leave The Gang without taking a Passout. A Passout is what you take when you have to go away for a while. Say your folks are going on a trip and they couldn't afford to be without you. Your old man's

Rock Hill

got a bad heart and you have to be on guard in case you have to grab the wheel if he has an attack on the road while going ninety miles an hour. You take a Passout so you won't lose your place in The Gang. That's how you still get to work up. You don't get to be an Officer overnight, you know!

Murderin' Sam says if you miss a meeting or a battle, you just might miss a chance to get promoted. I would never say good-bye. I mean, good-bye never means much anyway. It's just a bunch of hogwash to me. I mean, there are always tears and that sort of thing. That's one thing you're never ever going to see me do, no sir, I'll never cry. Crying is for babies and girls. Although to tell the truth, I did cry a lot one time when my dog Zip got killed when he was hit by a car. Boy I thought I was never gonna get over that, it really hurt! My Mom really helped me through that ordeal. She read me a poem about *"Rainbow Bridge"* where Zippy is waiting for me. Boy, sometimes I think I can't wait to play with Zip again!

⌘ ⌘ ⌘

Rainbow Bridge   Poem
Just this side of heaven is a place called Rainbow Bridge. When an animal dies that has been especially close to someone here, that pet goes to Rainbow Bridge. There are meadows and hill for all of our special friends so They can run and play together. There is plenty of food, water and sunshine, and our friends are warm and comfortable.
All the animals who had been ill and old are restored to health and vigor. Those who were hurt or maimed are made whole and strong again, just

as we remember them in our dreams of days and times gone by. The animals are happy and content, except for one small thing: they each miss someone very special to them, who had to be left behind. They all run and play together,
but the day comes when one suddenly stops and looks into the distance. His bright eyes are intent. His eager body quivers. Suddenly he begins to run from
the group, flying over the green grass, his legs carrying him faster and faster. You have been spotted, and when you and your special friend finally meet, you
cling together in joyous reunion, never to be parted again. The happy kisses rain upon your face; your hands again caress the beloved head, and you look once more into the trusting eyes of your pet, so long gone from your life but never absent from your heart.
Then you cross Rainbow Bridge together ...
Author unknown ...

⌘ ⌘ ⌘

Dad says a real man always has to take the bad with the good. He says, "Thank heavens there is more good than bad in life. But sometimes tears will flow. When they do, that is when a man has to handle his problems with - Character. A Little Sweat Off The Brow, a Steady Hand and A Man's Brains are the best solutions to any problem a person can have." Gee, my Dad is a very smart man!

I can see it now. After I miss a few meetings and no one sees me around, pretty soon some of the guys will start checking.

When they all learn that I really did leave for sure, they might even vote me a Mosquito Blood Brothers Bravery Badge like we voted Murderin' Sam when he killed those three hundred Japanese Dive Bombers in one evening's time. Actually, they were only flying ants, but we called them Japanese Dive Bombers and pretended the ants were attacking our homeland like the sneaky Japs did at Pearl Harbor. Our Mosquito Blood Brothers Bravery Badges are actually shoulder patches that we get from the local gasoline service stations. Mr. Horton who owns the Mobil station gives us patches that show the "Flying Red Horse" logo, Mr. Damer's son, Elton, who owns the Union 76 station gives us patches with the "76" logo, and Mr. Mires, who owns the Associated Station, gives us patches with a "Flying A."

We also get as many Military patches as we can possibly get from World War II Veterans. My two proudest possessions are a patch from the US Army Eighth Air Force and a Screaming Eagle patch worn by the US Army 101st Airborne Division. Boy, are they terrific! When someone in The Gang does something that Murderin' Sam thinks is really great, we put it to a vote whether to award another patch or not to that member. Everyone in The Gang votes on who has earned the right to add another patch.

When one of the guys works up enough courage to come right out and ask my folks where I've gone, they'll really see something. What will probably happen is that Murderin' Sam and Tiger Terry will put Sleepy John and Wailing Willie in charge of asking my folks. They'll say that those guys have to do it because they're still proving that they got the stuff to be Mosquito Blood Brothers. They are, too; I mean, they're not full-blooded Mosquito Blood Brothers yet, you know. That takes a while. Even I am not that far yet. I think they're only half bloods. Murderin' Sam says I'm just a quarter blood but coming on strong! I can just see my folks when they ask 'em where I've gone. They'll take on like they did at Uncle Bob's funeral. They'll wail and moan and it will really be awful. I'd kinda like to be sitting in the upstairs window in the house across the street watching. I'll bet it would really get sickening. I mean tears and all.

I'll bet you think that I wouldn't run away from home, either. Well, you're wrong. It wouldn't be hard. I'd run away in a minute if I had a brother to go with me. I'll tell you what we'd do. You know how big guys ride freight trains? OK, that's what we'd do. There sure isn't anything hard about riding freight trains, I'll tell you. I've heard my Uncles talk about it. I guess they rode a lot of them during the Great Depression, when men traveled all over the country looking for work. All you gotta do is watch how you get on and get off. That's how lots of guys get it. They don't watch good enough. They fall on the tracks and the train wheels just slice'em in two. Just think of the different number of boxcars that you'd get to ride on. Maybe if you got lucky on the trip, you might even get to ride in the caboose.

Say if somehow the guy that runs the train comes up on you while you were in a boxcar sleeping and he asks you who you are and where you're going, say he offered to give you a hot cup of cocoa to drink back in the caboose. You'd say yes and away you'd go. I mean, it could happen. You never know until you try, do you? There'd you be, seeing all kinds of country and meeting new people and everything. That would be the life. Course what would really be great is if The Gang could take off and live like that. But that'd never happen because most of them would be too afraid to ever leave home. Why, even Murderin' Sam said that most of The Gang would be too afraid to go walking in the light of the fullest moon up in the old town graveyard. I believe it, too. Most wouldn't dare.

When you get hungry on the trip, there'd be nothing to getting something to eat. You'd just get off and gather berries or shoot a bird with your slingshot or BB gun if you had your BB gun. (I have a real Red Rider model my Dad gave me for Christmas one year.) If you were in a city, then you'd just go looking for a job: cutting lawns, raking leaves, or washing dishes, even, I mean, if a guy's gotta, he's gotta. Washing dishes is better than starving to death, you know.

Of course you couldn't stay away forever. I mean, you'd have to come home after a while. You couldn't just stay away all the time. Why, your folks might send the FBI or the National Guard after you. Then you really would be in trouble. Oh, you could stay away from them for a while without being caught, but they're bound to catch up with you. They would set up train blocks and check for identity papers just like in those Gestapo movies that play at the Z Theater. You'd have to even watch who you talked to. You'd never know who might turn you in. They might even put up a reward for your arrest. Why, everyone might be on the lookout. Then you really would be in trouble. I mean, you couldn't trust anyone. You might even have to watch your own brother. I mean, watch what he says to strangers. Why, he'd give you away in a minute if you didn't watch him. He'd be talking to someone real simple like and then he'd blurt out that you'd run away from home and that you were never going back, and then you really would be in trouble.

Why, we'd have more guys on our neck than you could shake a Snooker Stick at. A Snooker Stick is what we use in The Gang to tell if a guy's got any diseases on 'em that you can't see. I never will forget old Wailing Willie, when Murderin' Sam and Hacksaw Harry found those diseases on Willie after we had a battle one time. You shoulda heard old Willie. He really went wild. You see, it works like this. If they find something on you with the Snooker Stick, they gotta fix it right then. Cause if they don't, why, you might die.

The only sure way they can fix it is to rub Magic Stinging Nettle Leaves on the place where you got it. Hacksaw Harry held Willie down and Murderin' Sam rubbed the leaves on him. Sam always says it's harder on him than it is the guy he's doing it to. I believe it, too. I mean they've had to do it to

Rock Hill

me lots of times, and you can just see it really hurts old Murderin' Sam to have to rub'em on you. He screws up his face and kinda gets tight all over and it really hurts him. You can really see it. Anyway, Sam and Harry really gave it to Willie because they said he had a real bad case. Murderin' Sam said Willie had such a bad case of whatever he had that it almost broke the Snooker Stick right in two. Boy, did Willie scream. It was really awful. But he shut up after about a half hour, and like we told him, he mighta been dead if it hadn't been for the Magic Stinging Needle Leaves.

When you did decide to come home, you can just imagine what the folks would say. I'll bet they would really be surprised if suddenly there you were walking up the sidewalk. Maybe by then you'd have grown a beard or something and they wouldn't know you at first. I mean you might stay away that long. Who knows? Maybe they'd throw a party for you and invite the neighbors and all The Gang. You'd get to do everything with no one being against you. Boy, that would be great! If someone came that you didn't like, why you could just tell him to leave and be quick about it or you might take off again. It would almost be like being a King!

Yes, I know it for sure. A girl never would fit in. That's certain. Take Dad, for example. He always says there's nothing he'd like better than to have two boys to get into his things like I do. I mean, you know he's always kidding, but he likes me. Even when he's mad, he likes me. I can always tell. And Mom? Well, Mom's Mom. I mean, she's that way. Sometimes

I think that she would like me even if I were a girl. I mean I'm not, and I never want to be either, but I'm just saying if I were.

Let me ask you a question. Take my toys. All of them. What toys of mine could I give my sister? Unless you consider a blackboard or a beach ball or a pair of skates as toys for girls, there is not a girl's toy in the whole bunch. I sure couldn't give her my fielder's glove (a real broken-in trapper model) or my US Army battle helmet or my Mosquito Blood Brother Badges to a girl. Never in a million years. She wouldn't know how to take care of them.

Just take the simple trick of rubbing a glove with Neatsfoot Oil after you use it. Why, there is not a girl in the whole world who would think of doing that and you know it. I can just see it. A girl would take my glove out and use it and chances are, she wouldn't even ask me. She would just take it. She wouldn't bother to warm up the glove, let alone her arm. I mean it's only fair: you can only expect a glove to do so much. Before the day was over she'd drop it in the dust or kick it or throw it because she was too dumb to know how to catch a grounder or a fly. If you tried to teach her, she'd probably get angry and just say you were only trying to act smart. Then that would only make me angry. You know what happens when I get angry? I just go off by myself and I don't say a word to anyone about why or where I'm going. Oh, I'd probably talk to her all right, but I mean not out loud. I might even call her some Mosquito Blood Brothers Mad Monikers, too. Right here I better tell you what a Mad Moniker is cause if I don't, you'd think I was talking through my battle helmet. A Mad Moniker is what the Mosquito Blood Brothers call the real bad words that we use. I mean, we don't use them all the time. We might get thrown in jail or asked to leave the country if we used them all the time. We only use them when we're really angry at someone. We ain't the first ones to use them either. We just like to think that we help keep them going. I mean, you know, so they won't be forgotten.

⌘ ⌘ ⌘

I didn't tell you why I'm out here today, did I? Heck, I haven't even told you where I am. Well, I'm up on the actual Rock Hill Rock because my Mom wouldn't let me go camping with the rest of The Gang. I am sitting on the big rock that gives the town its name. Behind me is the number 1949 that the High School Seniors painted on the Rock to record the year of their graduation. Below me, I can see the wide valley with the town of Rock Hill sitting in the middle. I also see the grocery stores, Grange Hall, fire station, and the school buildings where I go to school.

Running through the town west to east, I see US Highway 12, which starts at Aberdeen near the Pacific Ocean and runs clear to Minneapolis, where my Teacher Miss

Charlotte Heart graduated from College. She says US Highway 12 continues on to the huge city of Chicago, known as the "Windy City," then to Detroit, known as the "Motor City." When Miss Heart said something about the "Windy City," Murderin' Sam looked at me and shouted at the top of his voice to the whole class, "That must be where Jim was born!" Even Miss Heart thought that was funny! Miss Heart says US Highway 12 is our motor route to adventure, mystery, and opportunity when we are older and smart enough to take advantage of our future.

Once in a while, when I am here by myself, I practice my grenade throws. I'll pick up a rock and throw it just as far as I can. I never do hit anything. I mean, say I aim at a truck down on US Highway 12. I let it fly as far as I can, but so far the rock always falls short out in the brush somewhere. It never

Rock Hill Valley & US Highway 12 – Year 1949

Rock Hill

really goes very far. I always think the rock will hit the target, but it hasn't yet. Dad says, "Your arm's not strong enough yet, but that is no reason to quit. You must practice, practice, practice. Practice will always make you better." It is like my Teacher Miss Heart says, "Set a goal, aim high, and always keep striving to succeed."

Up on Rock Hill Rock, I pretend to see the future. I know you really can't, but it's fun to imagine what you'll be doing when you're grown up and moved away. Sometimes I see myself playing sports for a living or even being a Coach of a famous team. Sometimes I imagine what it's like to be a United Airline Pilot or a US Army Officer. I really can't wait to be grown up and living in some exciting place doing a job worthwhile. I would really like to help others. That would be great! If I look really hard, I can see my room in the school. I can see my desk and the wall board where Miss Heart posted my drawing of an airport with military planes, soldiers, and the United States Flag waving proudly. Miss Heart said I had earned the posting because I had been good in class. I mean, I'm never really bad. It's just that she says I like to talk too much during class. She said I had been quieter on that day than I had on other days so she put my picture up. It was a good one, too. Even she said that.

I better tell you about Miss Heart. She is the best Teacher a guy could have. She is so nice and smart. She really makes me feel like I could be somebody important someday. She's also the prettiest Teacher I've ever had. With apologies to

Dixie and my Mom, Miss Heart is the best-looking girl I know. Even my Dad says she really is a looker. He says, "She's the blonde knockout from the land of sky-blue waters." Whatever that means? She has long, blonde hair she mostly wears in a palomino pony tail, beautiful blue eyes that sparkle like real stars hanging on a Christmas tree, and a cute little nose that looks just like the one on a precious china doll my Grandmother has. Her skin is something to see! It is pure white, like a cake of bar soap, and her hands are so warm when she touches you. Yes, as far as girls go, Miss Heart is all right.

One other thing: maybe I shouldn't say this, but it always makes me mad when some jerk has to say something bad about something good. One time Phil Olson heard me bragging about Miss Heart, and he said, "Yeah, and she's got two pretty good size grapefruits hanging on her chest, too." Geez, I could have smacked him for that. I would have, too, if I'd had a rock, but he's a big fellow and **my Dad says, "A guy has to be not only prepared but very careful HOW, WHEN, and WHERE he defends his territory. Plus, do not forget 'WHY,' which is the most important reason. You must make sure you are in the right and your feet are standing on honorable ground before you take action. Always remember one other important fact: Sometimes an action causes a reaction. You must always be prepared for life's surprises!"** Anyway, I told Murderin' Sam what the Olson kid said, and Sam said, "It was a good thing I wasn't around to hear him say it, I would have kicked the living you-know-what out of him." Sam would have, too. You get on the downhill side of Sam and you're in for a tough time, I'll say. You just never know what Murderin' Sam will do or think up.

One hot summer day I saw Murderin' Sam talk a city kid who was visiting his Grandmother into peeing in a bottle and then drinking it. Sam told the city kid it would taste just like root beer soda pop: sweet and just a little bit warm. After peeing in the bottle, the city kid tried to back out, but Sam wouldn't let him. He threatened the city kid with being thrown on a hornet's nest if he didn't do it. Boy, it was really funny. You should have seen that kid's face when he tasted the first swallow. He must have spit and gagged for thirty minutes afterward. Of course, wouldn't you know, the little twerp ran home to his Grandmother as quickly as he could, told on us, and we all got in trouble over that deal. I had to stay in my yard for a whole week just to pay "penance," as my Mom said. When Murderin' Sam's Dad heard about the little joke, Sam said he lost a race with his old man's leather strap.

One thing for sure, though, we never saw that city kid around again the rest of that summer. Murderin' Sam said it was a good thing, too, because if Sam had caught him out he would have stomped the little varmint for causing Sam's Dad to give him what his old man joyfully called, "one of life's little lessons." I feel bad for Sam because his Dad really whips him hard sometimes. Sam says one of these days he's going to show his Dad a thing or two, and I really believe he will someday.

One time when The Gang was all together, we asked Sam when his Dad had whipped him the hardest. He said it was the time when Sam and his older brother had got into it while they were taking a bath together. Being poor, his folks rationed the heated bath water. Sam said his brother was being a total jerk. I guess the brother was hogging the soap and washcloth and splashing water in Sam's face. Sam said to get back at his brother he decided to relieve himself in the bath water. He said he probably would have got away with the stunt if he had gone number one. Instead, he went number two. Sam said when the turd went sailing through the water like a German U-boat his brother let out a scream like he was being tortured by the Gestapo. His Dad came running into the bathroom to see what was going on. Sam said it didn't take his Dad long to figure out what Sam had just done - or for his Dad to get the leather strap to cure Sam of what his Dad called, "A serious case of outright stupidity." Sam said when the lesson was over, he could not sit down for a week. We all believed him, too.

My reading has really improved in Miss Heart's class. That's for sure. I really do like to read, especially books and stories about airplanes, sports, and animals. Miss Heart says reading lets a person learn about other people, places, and things they'd probably never get to see or know. She says it's a big picture window to the whole wide world. I really believe her. Some of the books I have read outside of the classroom are Mark Twain's *Huckleberry Finn* and *Tom Sawyer*. I had to do an oral book report on both books in front of the class. It was fun reading the stories of boys growing up and made me think how interesting it is to live by a great river where the boat traffic of the world floats by. In a way, Huckleberry, Tom, and I have that in common because when I go to my Grandpa's house during the summer, one of my jobs is to go sturgeon fishing with him along the Columbia River. Since a lot of time is spent waiting for a big fish to swallow a little smelt fish used for bait, I pass the time watching the huge ocean ships sail by. Some carry oil upriver to Portland; others carry American wheat and lumber down river to foreign countries. At the back of the ships, painted in large letters, you can read the home ports of the vessels. A lot of time the ships are from China, India and sometimes even Europe. I like to imagine what it would be like to someday visit those far - away places with such strange sounding names: Bombay, Hong Kong, Marseille, Rotterdam, and Liverpool are just a few.

One time, I asked Miss Heart if she ever traveled overseas. She said only in her dreams, which made the class laugh. She said that's why boys are sometimes luckier than girls. If their job doesn't cause them to travel, the Military does. I said I hoped to enjoy both. She said, "Good for you. Put your mind to an idea, work hard and long enough, and anything is possible." Miss Heart is one of the smartest people I know. I swear!

Sally Dunn, a girl in our class who has red hair and buckteeth, said to Miss Heart, "Maybe your boyfriend would take you overseas sometime." She smiled and said she would never trust her friend in a rowboat let alone on an ocean - going ship. The whole class thought that was funny. Another girl in the class, Connie Anderson, asked Miss Heart if she had any brothers or sisters. Miss Heart said she did, six sisters and one brother. Miss Heart also told us that two of her sisters, Ginny and Vi, were beautiful enough to be movie stars! She also said that her sister Ginny's husband was a heroic US Air Force pilot who set speed records in his jet fighter. Wow, I wanted to learn more about him! Finally, Miss Heart said Vi's husband was a very successful operator of an Elixir Emporium whose inventory was of such variety that the store sold products fit for Kings, Queens, and even Savages, believe it or not.

That night I told Mom and Dad what Miss Heart said about her Family. Mom said, "As lovely as Miss Heart is, her Family must be beautiful and her Parents must make a handsome couple." Dad said, "Such beauty is surely temptation equal to Cleopatra. While I am not interested in the Emporium's merchandise, I do employ a bunch of loggers who on weekends would probably drink the establishment dry!"

Three other books I really liked are *My Friend Flicka* and *Thunderhead by Author Ms Mary O'Hara and Black Beauty by Author Ms Anna Sewell*. Wow, talk about terrific stories about horses and a boy's love for them. It was great to learn about Wyoming and ranching, too. I think if a guy ever got a chance to live like a cowboy it would be something. Someday I would like to live in Wyoming, that is for sure! Mom and I read the books together. It really helps to have your Mother join in the reading session. I feel sorry for other kids whose folks don't read with them. Mom really liked the three books as well, especially the parts about the boy's Mom and Dad in *My Friend Flicka* and *Thunderhead*. The Dad had been an Officer in the US Army, a graduate of West Point. The Mother was from an important Family from the East Coast of the United States. They shared the struggles of running the ranch and went to barn dances for fun on Saturday nights. Mom said it was obvious they really loved each other. I said, "Just like you and Dad, right?" She said, "Right, but unlike her husband, your Dad does not like to dance at all!"

The book *Black Beauty* was written by English Author Anna Sewell. Boy, that is a terrific book for sure! It's a story about horses used for pulling carriages and wagons before the use of the automobile. Told through the eyes, brains and mouth of *Black Beauty*, the horse himself, it's a tale of the treatment of horses by their owners, or caretakers. Reading what *Black Beauty* thought and had to say, I wondered just who the dumb animals really were anyway – Horses or Humans?

Some owners treated their horses like they were their own children, and cared for them with true love and respect; other men were unbelievably cruel and considered the horse only as a work tool.

Sprinkled throughout the book *Black Beauty* by Author Ms Sewell, who wrote the terrific story while an invalid in the last years of her life, were quotes from the Holy Bible which offered rules for living one's life: Mom said these rules applied for adults as well as boys and girls.

Once in the *Black Beauty* story, the Groomsman John witnessed a boy treating a horse with cruelty. "Cruelty", John said, "was the Devil's own trademark. I say anyone taking pleasure in cruelty, we know who he belongs to. The Devil was a murderer from the beginning, and a tormentor to the end. On the other hand, when we see people who love their neighbors and are kind to man and beast, we know that is God's mark, for God is love. There is no religion without love and people may talk as much as they like about their religion, but if it does not teach them to be good to man and beast, it is all a sham."

Mom said, "Remember, Jim, all animals are God's creatures, too. The love your dog "Zip" gave you was heaven sent. When you two meet again over Rainbow Bridge, the love and joy you once showed each other will be rekindled through our Heavenly Father. Never forget – an animal's love for his master is a precious and Holy gift and God expects Man to reciprocate."

See what I mean about books? I think Miss Heart is right. She says, "Learn how to read and you can learn from the thoughts of others. If a person doesn't know how to read, it is like being blind to the world around you!" I'm so thankful that Miss Heart came into my life. I don't think I can ever thank her enough. I never want a girl and I never ever want to get married, but if I ever had a girl and ever did get married, I would want someone just like her. Dad says, "Miss Heart is the stuff real logger's dreams are made of. It's going to be one lucky guy who wins her heart."

⌘ ⌘ ⌘

For now, my dreams are about Aviation and my role as a Pilot. Miss Heart has encouraged my interest in flying. She says I'd make a great Pilot. She said I reminded her of a guy who once took her for a ride in a biplane. With a laugh she said the Pilot was always trying to get her upside down just to hear her scream. The whole class laughed and thought that must have been exciting! As much as I like Miss Heart, though, most girls can't tell an airplane from a Blue Jay. How on earth could a guy ever carry on a conversation with a girl about how many bombs a B-29 can carry? A girl wouldn't know and, what's worse, wouldn't care.

Rock Hill has a short grass strip for its airport. It's down on the prairie, west of town. I go there quite often. Many in The Gang do, too, but they don't have the same interest. I plan to be a Professional Pilot some day. I'd like to fly all over the world either as a Pilot in the Military or for an airline. At our airport, we have an Aeronca Champion, a Piper Cub, a Stinson Voyager, a Navion, and a US Army Air Force Consolidated Vultee BT-13 Trainer - nicknamed The Valiant. The Valiant doesn't fly because it doesn't have an engine, although I sit in the cockpit sometimes and pretend it does! Most of the Pilots are guys who learned to fly in the Military. They are a great bunch of people and now just fly for fun.

Will Stone, my good friend, owns the Aeronca Champion. I met Will and his wife, Pauline, when Will was selling rides at the Rock Hill Pioneer Days Celebration: five dollars for fifteen minutes. Dad and Mom said yes to my request for a ride and away Will and I flew. One flight and I was hooked for life. It was fantastic. I couldn't believe how small and clean everything looked from up in the air. It was like seeing a whole new world for the first time. Right from the first flight, Will and I liked each other. He let me handle the stick and adjust the throttle, which was by the window on the left side of the red and yellow Champion. Will pointed out the rudder pedals on the floor, but my legs were too short to reach them. After that first fifteen - minute flight, Will could tell I had a special feeling for flying. He said I could

Rock Hill

come to the airport anytime. I was so thrilled that the next day I walked the mile to the grass strip. It was the start of a lifelong friendship, between Will and me and a serious love affair with aviation.

I wash planes and have learned the proper way to push on the wing struts to help park them. The great thing is I get to go for rides anytime there is an empty seat available. Hacksaw Harry, my best friend and one of the members of The Gang, likes to help the Aircraft Mechanics by cleaning the tie - down area and dumping garbage. He gets to go for free rides too but says that he would rather work on the planes than fly them. One time Harry beamed when Will winked at me and said, "Aircraft Mechanics are even more important than Pilots! It's dangerous to fly an airplane that's not maintained properly on a regular basis."

Saturday and Sunday are the really busy days at the airport with lots of takeoffs and landings. People come from all over the area to watch the activity. Will Stone says every American Family might have an airplane to match the Family car some day. I asked my Dad if he would take flying lessons, but he just smiled and said he would leave that for me to do.

At the school library I read *Flying* magazine. Mom subscribed to *Air Facts* for me. The guy who sold us the subscription was a World War II Vet with hooks for hands who came to our door. Dad said it was a damn shame our Country could not do more for Heroes like him. The Salesman just smiled and said, "Thanks," and shook my hand as he left. It felt funny shaking hands with a hook. I told Murderin' Sam about it and he said he once shook hands with a pirate with a hook at a carnival. Sam said he thought it would be neat to have a hook, but I didn't.

One time I wrote the Cessna and Beechcraft Aircraft Manufacturing Companies in Kansas for free literature offered in their magazine ads. Boy oh boy, you wouldn't believe what they sent me. Full - color brochures with pictures of Cessna 120s, 140s, 170s, and 195s. The Beechcraft Company sent me a large photograph of their Bonanza, it is a four - seat plane with a special "butterfly" tail that is used for business and personal flying. The Beechcraft Bonanza is a special favorite of mine. Last summer our Family drove right by the Beechcraft factory in Wichita, Kansas, on our way to Missouri to visit relatives. There must have been over a hundred new Bonanzas sitting by the runway. I went to sleep that night counting Beechcraft Bonanzas instead of sheep.

We were gone for six weeks on that trip, and I sure missed The Gang. Hacksaw Harry said it was really quiet with me gone. It had been almost twenty years since my Mother and her Family had moved west. Mom said they had lots of food to eat in Missouri since they lived in the country and always had a garden, but the Family was poor as Church Mice and suffered financially during the Great Depression. Three Model Ts and four Families made the trek west together. Dad says Mom's Family were the original Joads.   Whoever they are?

Rock Hill

After arriving in Washington State, most stayed in Longview. But, because of a shortage of jobs during the Great Depression, some Uncles and Aunts headed south to Fresno, California to work in the grape fields.

Several times a year a US Air Force Beechcraft D18 twin- engine trainer from McChord Air Force Base in Tacoma buzzes our field at over two hundred miles an hour at least. It's really exciting. The engines are very loud. The US Air Force Pilots gain altitude, slow up, and go around to act like they're going to land on Rock Hill's little airstrip. The Pilots drop the flaps, lower the wheels, and at the right moment, just before touchdown, gun their engines to take off again. The Military Pilots attract quite a crowd. The Gang stands at attention and salutes as the plane flies by. Will Stone, who was never in the Military, says someday, somewhere, some enemy is going to pay a high price for challenging their flying skills. These United States Air Force Pilots are awfully good!

One of the best things about living in Rock Hill is that the town lies directly underneath the flight path of the main north/south airline routes. On a clear day, the West Coast, United, and Northwest Orient Airlines DC3s, DC6s, and DC7s are visible overhead. Some flights are short hops between Portland and Seattle; others are flights headed for California. I dream all the time about being the Captain of such an Airliner.

ELEMENTARY SCHOOL

Beechcraft Bonanza
photo courtesy of Beechcraft Corporation

Rock Hill

Sometimes when The Gang is out on patrol, we all look at the airplanes using Murderin' Sam's binoculars. One day we saw a Pan American Clipper that was bound for Seattle and then on to Alaska. My Dad says that Pan American Pilots are the cream of the crop. Dad flies on Pan American planes whenever he can. I once read a book called *Under My Wings* by Basil L. Rowe, Pan American Airline's Chief Pilot. He was written up in *Ripley's Believe It or Not* as having the most hours and air mileage of any living Pilot. He sounded like a terrific person full of flying knowledge and aerial wisdom. His Pilot License was signed by Wilbur Wright and he had been an Air Race Pilot when flying was just beginning. It is interesting how reading about someone else's life can inspire a person. I believe if a guy doesn't learn about anything else in school, he should learn how to read. Miss Heart says a guy will have a greater chance at success in life by following in the literary footsteps of others by reading about their lives and experiences.

It rains a lot in Rock Hill so the skies and the Airliners are obscured at night much of the time. In the dark, you only hear the Airliners flying overhead, their big engines droning loudly through the air. Sometimes I wonder if they are flying "in the soup," as Will Stone says, or "flying above the clouds." Either way, the Airliners all fly IFR: Instrument Flight Rules. When the weather is bad, most of the Pilots on our field fly what Will calls "IFRRET"— I Follow Railroads Except for Tunnels. Will Stone says, "If you truly wish to be a Professional Pilot, you are going to have to learn how to fly using only instruments. A Professional Pilot has to be capable of flying all hours in any weather when duty calls and government weathermen say flying is safe."

On clear nights, it's a beautiful sight to see the Airliners passing Rock Hill overhead as well. It's easy to spot their red and green wing tip lights. As they disappear, the white light on their tails twinkles good- bye. Andy Weld, a new kid in school, said Winlock, the town where he came from, sat by the railroad tracks. Union Pacific Trains were always going by night and day. He said he liked to watch the trains and dream about traveling somewhere on them. He said he liked to lie in bed at night and listen to the train whistle calling his restless feet. I said I felt the same way about the Airliners that passed overhead. I said sometimes I thought the roar of an aircraft engine was a call to get moving and do something worthwhile with my life. It's funny how the urge to leave Rock Hill is tied in with hearing a message in my mind to climb aboard and fly away to adventure and success in life.

Once, my Mom and Dad took me to an Air Show in Longview. The Aerocar was being built there. Dad said, "The city fathers are beating the sales drum." I really enjoyed the afternoon. There must have been a couple of thousand people there. The main act was the Ball - Ralston Flying Circus with their thrilling aerial performances in North American T-6 trainers. Sammy Mason from California awed the crowd by performing aerobatics in his Stearman Biplane. We also saw a World War II Vet with paralyzed legs fly a type of low - wing airplane called an Aircoupe that had no rudder pedals. Rudder control was tied in with the aileron control wheel on the instrument panel. He had a monkey for a co-pilot, which I thought was great. I told my Mom I wanted to get a monkey for a pet someday, but she said, "No way. One monkey in the Family is enough, thank you."

Mr. Molt Taylor's Aerocar was the star of the day. It was a real Airplane and a real car at the same time. When the Pilot flew into town, the wings, propeller, and tail could stay at the airport. The Pilot could then drive all over town. Or the Pilot could pull the Airplane portion of the plane behind the car. When he was ready to leave, he would reattach the wings, propeller, and tail back to the car and then fly away. It was almost unbelievable. When I told The Gang about the Aerocar, they thought I was pulling their legs. I said, "I am going to own one someday." They all laughed. Miss Heart doesn't ever laugh at me, though. She says, "A guy can have almost anything he wants and be almost anything he wants to be. He just has to be willing to pay the going price for success. The challenge is to know the cost and get prepared so you can afford to pay the bill.

*The car portion of the Aerocar Jim once owned can be seen at the
Seattle Museum of Flight.
It was upgraded by Mr. Molt Taylor, the Builder.*

⌘ ⌘ ⌘

I'll bet you'd never guess that I've won a school sales contest. Well I have! The whole school was selling magazine subscriptions

Rock Hill

and everyone got a textbook cover with the pictures of all the Presidents of the United States for just participating. I won the top prize: a one-hundred-dollar U.S. Savings Bond.

We were selling subscriptions for the Curtis Publications Company of Philadelphia, Pennsylvania. Miss Heart said that city was where the Declaration of Independence was signed by our Country's forefathers. It made us feel like we had a connection to those famous Americans who gave us our Country's Constitution and the Bill of Rights. My Dad said, "The City of Brotherly Love continues to have an impact on little old Rock Hill." The Gang worked really hard to be the best-selling class in the school. The contest ran for almost a month. I went all over Rock Hill to sell magazine subscriptions. People were very nice to listen to my sales story. Our school Principal, Mr. Don, and Miss Heart had helped us with a little outline on why the school supported the campaign: the school would receive money to buy teaching materials. The more magazines subscriptions sold; the more materials they could purchase. Plus, every student got a pencil and a writing pad for selling just one subscription.

The magazines were really easy to sell. Usually a Family bought a subscription to either the *Saturday Evening Post* (which Miss Heart said, "was founded by Ben Franklin," believe it not), *Country Gentlemen,* or *Holiday* magazine. If they were not interested in those magazines, then I asked if the man or woman in the house had a hobby, for there was surely a hobby magazine on the list to whet their interest. I really like calling on people. It is fun. My Mom says I am a natural-born go-getter. My Dad calls me "Salesman Sam." My Mom even hauled me around in the Family car to call on people outside of the town. **Mr. Don says I would probably make a great Salesman someday. He also said, "The world would come to a standstill unless some Salesman somewhere sold something to someone else; our great Country is built on a Salesman's ability to persuade. You must always remember to fill a genuine need with a quality product at a fair price." In his opinion: "There will always be room in this great Country for an HONEST Salesman who can help another person get what he wants when he needs it."**

When the contest was over, I had sold over one thousand dollars' worth of magazine subscriptions! The school had a special recognition ceremony where students received their awards. I was called up front last and was given a one hundred dollar US Savings Bond and a small Medallion with the image of Ben Franklin on it that hung around my neck. Mr. Don said I was surely headed for success as a Salesman someday in the future; Miss Heart actually shook my hand and gave me a hug. Boy, did she smell good, too! She said I was a Sales Superstar and was glad to have me represent her class so well.

Murderin' Sam also says he knew all the time I was going to come in first. The next time we got together The Gang all saluted me and voted me another Mosquito Blood Brother Badge. Murderin Sam also said I had won the right to carry the Mosquito Blood Brother Map Case for a whole month. See, we have all our battle and treasure maps in a brown leather case that's marked *Top Secret* on it. Usually, Murderin' Sam himself carries it and heaven help anyone who touches it without his permission. But Murderin' Sam said I

Rock Hill

had honored The Gang and The Gang should honor me, too. I was really proud.

⌘ ⌘ ⌘

One of my favorite hours at school is lunchtime. Along with others, I get to lead the class for lunch. The cafeteria is located in the basement of the Elementary School building. The Gang loves the food prepared and served by the friendly cooks and servers. Like Miss Heart says, "It is hot, delicious, and nutritious." Mrs. Mable Hedman is chief cook, five feet tall, and the wife of Mr. Tom Hedman, the Chief Mechanic/General Manager of the School Bus Garage and Transportation System. Their son, Mac, is a local Pilot and Log Truck Driver who treats me like I am a "Fellow of the Aerial Brethren". Every time I go to lunch I can expect a friendly smile from Mrs. Hedman. We go to the lunchroom by grade: first grade at 11:00 a.m. second grade at 11:10 a.m., and so on. High School students are the last at noon with lunch over at 1:00 p.m. Each grade is marched to the cafeteria in files of two; no talking in the hallways, no horseplay of any kind, or recess privileges are suspended for a day. We sit on benches facing long tables after passing single file through the food line. Food dishes are placed on trays. Talking is allowed while eating as long as we don't make too much noise. No funny business is tolerated: no throwing of food, no messing with anyone else's tray. Actually, we are so hungry that mischief is the furthest thing from our minds. We have twenty minutes to eat, then back to the classroom just before noon recess.

A hot lunch costs twenty cents. Mom gives me four dollars on the first day of each month to purchase a school hot lunch card that is good for one month. We keep the cards in our desks in the classroom. Miss Heart warns us everyday about taking good care of our card so we don't lose it. Also, she tells us how lucky we are to live in America where few go hungry and a free education is provided by the US Government.

Some of the poorer kids have to buy their lunch daily because their Parents can't afford to buy a card. Sometimes a few of the kids come to school without their lunch money; they always say they forgot it. Murderin' Sam does this a lot. Everyone in class knows it is just a lie, but Miss Heart, bless, her always has a solution. She says one of her main jobs as a Teacher is to create what she calls a "Genuine Emergency Fund." Miss Heart says she is responsible to the State of Washington to develop boys and girls who learn how to read, write, do math and more importantly, think. She says an empty stomach at lunch time can lead to a learning catastrophe: hunger pangs caused the brain to slip into "knowledge neutral" or, what's worse, "ignoramus anxiety." Miss Heart is required by the authorities to dip into her "Genuine Emergency Fund" to "loan twenty cents to any student who does not have hot lunch money." Isn't Miss Heart a wonderful person! I told my Mother about this policy one time. She said she'd bet Miss Heart never made much money on her loans but she probably got rich from her investments. I wasn't sure what she meant, but I liked the part where Mom said that at the next PTA meeting she would give Miss Heart five dollars to deposit into her "Genuine Emergency Fund" account. I said, "Thanks, Mom."

My favorite school hot lunch meal is chili, crackers, coleslaw, a sprig of grapes, milk, and chocolate cake with sweet white sugary icing about an inch thick. Boy oh boy, is it good. I could eat that meal everyday. We don't though because Miss Heart says the United States Department of Agriculture pays for a large share of our hot lunch program and the US Government requires the school to offer many different kinds of food.

Sometimes we have hamburgers with French fries; other times it is roast beef, mashed potatoes, and gravy or meatballs and spaghetti. There is always a salad along with a carton of milk. I can honestly say there isn't anything Mrs. Hedman and her helpers fix that I don't like. On second thought, my one complaint is ham and lima beans!

Some of the girls complain about the food, but The Gang all thinks they would complain about Coca-Cola our favorite drink, for heaven's sake! For some of the students the school lunch program provides the best-balanced, most wholesome food they eat. Miss Heart says the US Government is owed a debt of thanks for the school lunch program. Boys and girls all over America eat at least one well-balanced meal a day because of President Harry S. Truman, our US Senators, and Members of the House of Representatives. In fact, Miss Heart said, "Back in Minnesota my Family raises wheat on a farm that goes directly to the United States Government School Lunch Program." One day she had our class write the Honorable Russell V. Mack, our Representative in

Mom was a loving Mother who anchored the home and kept the fires burning while Dad worked away. She was an inspiration to all

Congress, thanking him for the food. He wrote us back, too. Miss Heart posted his letter on the school bulletin board for everyone to read. He said he and his colleagues would always work hard to continue and improve the school lunch program for hungry scholars striving to succeed in life.

Miss Heart says, "I hope some day the US Government will have a breakfast program to eliminate the hunger of unfortunate students whose Families are too poor to provide a wholesome breakfast prior to coming to school. It is impossible to study any subject when the mind is totally concentrating on an empty stomach. America is blessed with Farmers like my Parents who actually grow more food than this country can eat; yet, it is an American tragedy every day when some children go to school hungry."

Sometimes at recess when Miss Heart has to be the Recess Cop, I talk with her about life and other important things. She always listens and smiles and makes me feel like we share special thoughts that other people are unaware of. By the way, she is not a bossy cop on the playground. She's really very fair. Sometimes other Teachers act like they are G-Men with the FBI, for heavens sake! Especially when The Gang tries to get the dumb second grade boys to eat bugs. Murderin' Sam says we're only doing them a favor. He says some time in the future, they might get lost on a deserted island in the South Pacific. Then they would have to eat anything and everything that comes crawling by. "It's just practice for tough times ahead," Sam said.

One time after school I walked out with Miss Heart. On the sidewalk was a guy waiting for her. She introduced me to him. She said his name was Buddy. He was the friendliest person I ever met. He even shook my hand. Boy, was he swell! He thanked her for coming to him. She laughed and said she wasn't going to sprout wings and fly home. I thought that was funny. So did he. He said that since she looked like an Angel, he didn't see why she couldn't fly like one. Miss Heart just wrinkled her pretty china doll nose at him and said,

"Wouldn't you be surprised?!" Then he gave her a big hug. The way he looked at her was something to see. It was like he had been away for over fifty years and was seeing her again for the first time. I knew right then he knew what a special person my Teacher was. Yes sir, he was all right in my book, even if I saw him pat her butt with his hand!

That night at supper I told my Mom and Dad what happened. Mom smiled and said it looked like Miss Heart was lucky to have two fellows who were sweet on her. "Oh, Mom!" I said. My Dad said, "Buddy is her football-playing friend from college." Dad said he saw them together after a football game. They looked like they were very good friends. Dad also said, "For a guy his size, he is a pretty good football player, awfully rugged." I said, "He looked pretty big to me." Dad laughed and said, "He has a big heart anyway!" What that had to do with playing football I don't know.

One of the goofy girls in my class asked Miss Heart a really dumb question one day. She asked, "Are you going to marry your boyfriend?" Miss Heart laughed and said, "No, because I want a man who can carry the ball a little better and score a few more touchdowns." I wasn't sure what she meant so I told my Mom and Dad about it at supper. Dad laughed and said, "Miss Heart is going to learn someday that guys who just like to score touchdowns sometimes give themselves too much credit for their success. Anyway, truth be known, a great defense will beat a fancy offense any day." My Mom said something about "the importance of Character." I said, "Yes, that must be it. She thinks he's just a character." Mom put her hand on my shoulder, squeezed it, and I knew once again she was amazed about how smart I am sometimes.

A couple of times Mom and I have gone to the same Church as Miss Heart. **Mom says honoring and respecting other people's Religion and Beliefs is important. All people must learn and practice tolerance.** One Sunday morning Miss Heart had the football player with her in the pew in front of us. I watched them closely during the Service. The time in Church just flew by.

The football player was really something. I don't think he heard a word of the Sermon. He was looking at Miss Heart the entire time. He couldn't keep his eyes off her. During the part where we go up and down and up and down on our knees to pray, he had a big smile on his face. He really stared at her. Miss Heart took it just so long and then she, honest to God, gave him a punch in the side. She gave him a pretty good lick too. All he did was kind of smile a little bit. On the way out I heard the football player ask Miss Heart, "Why was the Priest swinging around that bee smoker up on the Altar?" I wasn't sure what he meant but she must have known. She laughed and darn if she didn't punch him hard again!

One time Murderin' Sam said he heard Miss Heart mutter something while he was facing the wall in the corner behind her desk. He said it was something about "not being satisfied with just a pot and a window." That night I asked Mom and Dad what she meant. They both snickered, and Dad said, "Even if you own a pot, some people are too lazy to dump it." Mom looked at Dad kind of funny and said, "Yes, well, some people who own windows always expect other people to keep them clean." Boy, was I in the dark about what they were saying to each other.

Now, you're probably wondering what old Murderin' Sam was doing standing in the corner. Let me tell you. Miss Heart was reading the class a great book about a pioneer Family that lived in the upper Midwest when our Country was young. The true story was about two girls name Laura and Mary and was really interesting. The Author of the tale was Laura Ingalls Wilder who had actually lived what she wrote about. Miss Heart says such writing makes for great reading and is the difference between fact and fantasy. Miss Heart also said that for a time, the Wilder Family lived in Eastern South Dakota, not too far from where she grew up in Southwest Minnesota.

All of a sudden, in midsentence, she jumped up to go flying down the aisle, only to stop at Murderin' Sam's desk. She looked right at him with those beautiful blue eyes that had turned to the color of gray slate and said, "Mr. Sammy Lawson Wilcox, did you make that awful smell in this classroom?" Murderin' Sam looked up at Miss Heart with a slight grin on his face and said, "Not me, Teacher, it must have been a dog that snuck in and out of the classroom without you seeing it."

With that answer, Hacksaw Harry laughed. Miss Heart glared at Harry and just dared him to laugh again. But old Harry knew better. The rest of us remained just as quiet as slugs to see what the end to this episode would be.

Wouldn't you know, Miss Heart showed what a wonderful person she is. She just took Sam by the ear, and, without managing to pull it off, she led him to the corner of the classroom by her desk. I will say, though, his ear was red as a strawberry when she finally let go of it. She ended the incident by telling Sam, "If you make any more smells - even one - during the rest of the entire school year, you will go directly to the Office for a Date with the Principal's Paddle."

Known to everyone in school as "Big Thunder," the paddle is a wicked-looking monster about two feet long and five inches wide with twenty holes drilled in it. Sam has met "Big Thunder" on more than one occasion. Once after "taking his medicine," as the Principal says, Sam said his butt looked like a waffle that his Mother had cooked too long. Miss Heart also said, "If 'Big Thunder' doesn't cure you of your rudeness, I will tell your Dad of your classroom interruption. I am sure your Dad would invite you to 'Dance The Jitterbug To The Leather-Strap Blues.'" It was apparent to all that Miss Heart had had a previous discussion with Murderin' Sam's Dad about Sam's classroom manners.

After school, The Gang all gathered around Murderin' Sam. Hacksaw Harry said, "Sam, you might have got away with it if you hadn't tried to blame it on a dog, for heaven's sake." Sam said, "Baloney." Then he went on to explain that his dog "Stupid" farted all the time, and, as a matter of fact, the dog farted so bad one time his Family was forced to vacate their home for a whole week. We all laughed at that claim, but Sam said it was true whether we wanted to believe it or not. He said one time his Mother threw out some barbecued beans that had gone bad into the garbage. "Stupid," who was part St. Bernard and part Mastiff, knocked over the garbage can, ate the beans with gusto, and then proceeded to gas the Family home a few hours later. As we headed to our homes, Hacksaw Harry asked Murderin' Sam to "show us a few quick jitterbug steps." Sam told Harry that he'd jitterbug on his head with a few left hooks if he didn't mind his own business and be quick about it.

⌘ ⌘ ⌘

An important position I hold this year at school is being a member of The Rock Hill School Safety Patrol. In the fifth grade I am just a guard; in the sixth grade I hope to be the Captain Of The Patrol, selected by Mr. Don, the Principal. The

Captain's job is to assign crosswalk positions to other guards and make sure everyone does his job properly. It is a real honor to be a member of the Rock Hill School Safety Patrol. My Dad

Rock Hill

says it's an opportunity for me to learn how important it is to have laws and require people to obey them. He says school safety patrol may be a pretty basic job, but if people don't follow rules, we all lose and someone might get hurt. At our school, without the safety patrol a student could get hit by a car. Our job is to help kids safely across streets while going to and from school. So far, our safety record is perfect.

All The Gang is on the patrol except for Murderin' Sam. He was, but Mr. Don removed him because he refused to let a parent cross the street one time when there wasn't any traffic coming. Sam claimed he was just doing his duty by showing her that he was the boss of the crosswalk. And, the rules require not dropping the red stop flag to halt traffic unless there are at least two people waiting to cross the street. Mr. Don and the parent, who, unfortunately for Sam, turned out to be the wife of a School Board member, said, "You were just being rude and a smart aleck." We all get to wear yellow vests with white belts and silver badges when the sun shines; on rainy days we also put on waterproof yellow slickers.

Miss Heart is the Teacher Supervisor of the Rock Hill School Safety Patrol. She is really good at her job. She taught us how to hold the red stop flags at the correct angle; how to always look out for first graders who might dash across the street without waiting for the flag to halt the traffic; and how to report older guys who either ignore the rules or give the Patrol or other kids a bad time.

That's another thing that got Murderin' Sam in trouble. On more than one morning he threatened to beat up a kid who either tried to run a stop flag or sass him. And he did a time or two. Actually, The Gang all thought most times the jerks had it coming. Like we said, Murderin' Sam probably saved their lives even if it cost a few knots on their heads. About his removal, Sam said it just gave him more time to sleep longer in the morning; plus, he always got his chores done at night before listening to "The Captain Midnight Program" on radio station KELA . He did say, "I do miss the candy toll." Occasionally, although it was definitely against the rules, Sam would charge a few first and second graders a piece of penny candy to cross the street.

For all the extra work we put in on School Safety Patrol, at the end of the year each member gets a Certificate of Achievement signed by the District Commander of the Washington State Patrol. It is really impressive, and my Mom and Dad said they would frame it for me. Also, in May, just before school is over for the year, School Safety Patrol Members from schools all over Western Washington are treated to an all-day picnic at Deep Lake Resort near Olympia, the State Capital. The Chief of the Washington State Patrol comes to give a talk to thank us all. It is really something! My Dad says the Washington State Patrol is one of America's premier law-enforcement organizations. The Chief's talk really made The Gang feel proud. He said that he would be unable to totally do his job without the help of all the members of the School Safety Patrol. It was almost like we, too, are a part of that famous group of Lawmen.

Rock Hill

⌘ ⌘ ⌘

I might as well tell you where I'm sitting. I'm sitting right in the middle of the Mosquito Blood Brothers Machine Gun Nest. I'm not supposed to be here unless there is an attack going on. We have 'em all the time. Oh they're not real ones, but they might as well be. The rest of The Gang is gone, so they'll never know that I am here. I can just see 'em. They're probably just about up to Ant Hill Junction by now. That's one of the places that The Gang uses for an outside meeting place. We named it Ant Hill Junction. Nobody else calls it that. Just us. We call it that because there are a couple of big anthills there. Once in a while we stop and watch them work and have a meeting. We poke the anthills with sticks and lob rock grenades on them. You should see them get mad. Boy, do they start moving around. They really go crazy!

Right now the guys are probably all moving kinda secret like so they won't be discovered. There's old Murderin' Sam in front leading the way. I'd bet you that he has that old pair of spyglasses that he got for fifteen Popsicle wrappers, and he's looking through them. Looking for enemy snipers, he always says. And he is, too. A guy never knows when he'll run into them on that trail. They're liable to be anywhere. You never know. Then right behind him is old Sleepy John. You gotta have Sleepy John right where you can keep your eye on him because he is liable to flake out anywhere. I really mean it. It wouldn't surprise me if that guy fell asleep on a pogo stick. The next guy that'd be walking up the trail is Tiger Terry.

He always walks behind Sleepy John. You see, that's one of his main jobs. That's part of him being a Mosquito Blood Brother. He's always got a stick in his hand and it's sharp on one end. Any time he thinks Sleepy John is about to hit dreamland, Tiger Terry just gives him a jab right square in the you-know-where. It really wakes him up, too. One time I saw Terry give him a jab and Sleepy John flew about three feet into the air. He looked like a rocket taking off. I always thought Terry poked John a little harder than necessary, but he darn sure never drifted off. The guy clear back in the tail end is Hacksaw Harry. That's where he always is. He has all his flags, books, and tools that he has to carry. He's even got a helmet with an antenna sticking out of the top of it. Of course it doesn't work, but he is always making like it does.

We have this system of signals that we use. Say, if the leader, Murderin' Sam, wants to know if we all want to stop to rest or make camp, why then he just goes, "HOOT HOOT HOOT HOOT." Kinda soft like. We all pass the word down to Harry, and if Harry thinks that it's safe to stop, like we're not being followed or something, then we stop. But if Harry starts going, "BEEP BEEP BEEP BEEP BEEP BEEP BEEP," then we know for sure it is not it safe to stop. We just keep going. Harry hasn't been wrong yet. When Hacksaw has said it was safe to stop, it always has been. We sure haven't run into any trouble yet.

By tonight they should be at Deadman's Creek where The Gang plans to spend the night. Actually, it's called Smith's Creek, but that's not what we call it. Murderin Sam says he

Rock Hill

doesn't know why everyone doesn't call it Deadman's Creek because there have been enough people who "got it" there. I can see why. There's quicksand, choke-moss, bitin' crickets, and fire ants and all kinda holes that you can't see over a hundred feet deep. It sure would be easy to meet what Dad calls "The Grim Reaper" there. One time I thought I was gonna get "The Grim Reaper" for sure, but The Gang got to me in time. See, Wailing Willie and I had gone after some wood to use for a fire to send Indian Smoke Signals with. Before I knew it, I had stepped into a hole that Murderin' Sam later said had already swallowed thirty men, a cow, and a baboon that had escaped from a circus. It was a close call, but I hung onto a root of an old stump until the rest of the guys reached me. Like they said, it took a lot of doing, but I did it. I hung on until they got there!

If it had not been for my Mom, I'd be there with 'em right now. I will tell you what happened. See, I came home from being uptown. To begin with, I wasn't supposed to be up there. We'd gone hunting for pop and beer bottles. We always find and sell 'em. Sometimes you're lucky and you find quite a few; other times you don't find any. The best time to look is after a dance. People throw 'em out of their cars. It pays pretty good, too. Sometimes you get a penny a piece and sometimes you get two cents. It all depends on what kind you find. When I got home, why, Mom really lit into me. I mean, you would have thought I was Hitler or Tojo or somebody like that! As I came into the kitchen where she was, Mom asked me, "Where have you been?" And I told her, "Out." And then she asked me,

"Out where?" Then, I said, "OUTSIDE!" And then she said, "Don't be a Smartmouth, Mr. Jim, Where have you been?" I told her, "Uptown," and then she said, "Why?" And finally, I had to tell her. And then, boy oh boy, she really blew a gasket. She went into that kick about me being an only child and having all the money I needed without having to hunt for beer and pop bottles. Then, Mom said that I couldn't go with The Gang for a whole week. That's when I said some things that I wouldn't have said if she hadn't said what she said.

I know Mom is overly protective of me because she thinks she is lucky to have me. Not that I'm special or anything. It's just when I was born I almost died. See, it was in 1938. We lived on a small farm in a rental thirty-five miles from a hospital. During the week my Dad was working and living at a logging camp a hundred miles away as a High Climber – a very important logger who cuts the tops out of trees, then rigs the "spar" trees for high-lead logging operations. The only transportation to the job and back was by steam railroad. He left for the camp on Sunday nights and returned home on Friday evenings.

Mom said Dad was lucky to have a job with so many men in the Country unemployed. He had no choice but to leave Mom under the care of her folks who lived five miles away. Anyway, when it came time for Mom to go to the hospital to have me, there was a delay in getting Mom to town. Once there, I guess she had a difficult delivery. I turned out to be a "blue baby," which had something to do with my heart and blood system. I guess it was touch and go for a while. Finally at three o'clock in the morning, the Doctors, as a last resort, gave me a shot of rye whiskey. With the Doctor's declaration, "We have done all we can. Now it is in the hands of God." Mom's loved ones were told to Pray. The Doctors stated, "If the boy lives through the night, he will probably survive."

At the same time, something occurred that changed my life. My Mom had a Sister-in-law who was a Christian Scientist. Aunt Jo contacted a lady called a Practitioner, and God's love and powers were requested. Lo and behold, I made it through the night. Having equated Prayer with my survival, from that time on my Mother was a Christian Scientist. When I got old enough to read, we read the Bible and Mary Baker Eddy's *Science and Health with Key to the Scriptures* together. We also subscribe to the *Christian Science Monitor*, which the whole Family reads with great interest. My Dad says the *Monitor* is considered by most thinking people to be one of the most well-written, authoritative papers in the world. Most Sunday mornings Mom and I drive thirty-five miles away to a Christian Science Church in Centralia for services.

One thing, though, my Dad believes Medicine and Science are gifts from God. Dad says, "Mom can pray all she wants, but if anyone in the Family gets sick or needs dental care or glasses, they are going to see a Doctor. My Family is always going to benefit from Health Professionals." Mom says she really and truly knows when Dad puts his foot down he means what he says, and she doesn't argue. Still, Mom maintains that regular Prayer and the study of the *Bible and Science and Health with Keys to the Scriptures* are the answers to a happy and fruitful life, relatively free of sickness, strife, and pain.

My Dad always quickly adds, "A positive attitude in life and a good healthy dose of hard meaningful work doesn't hurt either."

So here I am. All by myself. And you know, I just can't figure it out. My Mom hasn't been right lately. My Dad says that it's got something to do with the new baby, but I sure don't know. She sure doesn't treat me right these days. I think sometimes she gets out of bed just looking for me to do something wrong. Dad, too. You should hear the way she talks to him! I don't know how he keeps from running away. I really don't.

I'll bet you that when I get big and have a wife, if she ever talks bad to me, I'll just threaten to boot her in the rear end just like old Murderin' Sam did the Olson kid when he stole Sam's place in the Mosquito Blood Brothers Machine Gun Nest. I mean, Olson, why, he is not even a member of The Gang! We wouldn't let him join cause he's too dumb to be in it. Do you know what he said one time? "We oughta let girls be in The Gang." Right in front of everybody! REAL GIRLS, MIND YOU!

Then, there was that other thing, too. I remember it really well. I don't think I will ever forget it. Never! If I am dead, even! We were all at Deadman's Creek swimming, and the Olson kid said, "We oughta all take out our you-know-what's and see who has the longest one." I mean what a dumb thing to say! I thought old Murderin' Sam was gonna flip Olson's lid right there. Boy, Sam was mad! Olson said he was only kidding and didn't mean anything by it. Sam said, "OK but if you ever say anything like that again, I am gonna punch you right square in your big pimply face." Boy, has that Olson kid

Rock Hill

got pimples! One time Murderin' Sam said that it was getting hard to see Olson for the pimples. Hacksaw Harry said once Olson stayed all night with him because Harry said he wanted to count how many pimples Olson had. Harry said that he fell asleep at number 525. I believe it, too!

Tell you the truth, I don't see how Dad takes Mom's attitude toward him. I really don't. He always says some junk about Mom not feeling well. He tried to tell me one time about something I can't even remember and finally he gave up. I mean, not that I'm dumb or anything. It's just that I don't think Dad knew all about what he was saying. He used some big words named after some guy named Caesar and, heck, I'd never heard those words used before. I mean you sure can't blame me for not knowing what he was talking about, can you? The thing is, on days like today I just know Mom wants a girl. Cause I know that she knows that if she got a girl, she wouldn't have to worry about her wanting to go camping with The Gang or looking for bottles or staying overnight in a tree house!

Man, you should have heard her when she threw that fit about me wanting to stay all night in the tree house with The Gang! It sure wouldn't have hurt anything. We have everything made safe and solid. We got it all walled up except for peepholes that we need to look out of so you can see if anyone is coming. We also use the holes to put our guns out of. No, you sure can't fall out the sides. The floor is pretty good, too. Murderin' Sam fixed that. He left enough room for a guy to climb up the rope and then get into the tree house. We've got hooks to hang up our things. What we did was to drive in nails and then bend them over. The roof? Well that's the best part of it. There isn't any. That's what makes it so good. You can look up at the stars at night and you can almost see a billion miles away. That's what Murderin' Sam says anyway. It must be all of that because my Dad told me one time it took three whole years for the light from those stars to get here on earth. If I don't believe anyone else, I sure do believe Dad.

It's funny. When you are up in the tree house and it rains, the drops come right in on you. Those raindrops came a long way to hit in your tree house. It makes you feel important. It really does. Another thing that's funny is how our tree house changes from time to time. Like, you take now. It's summer. OK, the tree is full of leaves and it almost hides our tree house from the ground. It smells different, like things are growing, and they are. We each got us an apple that we're watching grow. Whoever has the biggest apple when they stop growing gets to look through the Rocketscope for a whole week. Since you probably don't know what a Rocketscope is, I better tell you. It's a couple of mirrors hooked up secret like in a wooden box so that you can look to see if it's safe to lower the rope. You wouldn't want to lower the rope if there was somebody down there you didn't like, would you?

Later in the year when the apples are ripe and the leaves are brown and yellow and red, why it's still different. You get shade in different spots than you ever did before, it will get dark earlier, and you'll have to go home sooner, and it will even smell different, too. Each day that you go there, you keep thinking that you're gonna go back and there's not gonna be anything left. Sometimes I wish this time of my life would last forever; I really do! I know it won't, but I really do feel that way sometimes.

We don't go out there much in the wintertime because it's too cold and the rope is too hard to hang onto. The tree looks so bare. It looks like it had been taking a shower in the rain, then somebody came by and swiped all of the tree's green-colored clothes when it wasn't looking. There it is shivering and waiting for spring to come around and bring it a new set of leaves.

I think that's when I like it the best: In the springtime. Everything always smells fresh, like a new pair of tennis shoes. It is surprising how things happen so fast. You go out and there is nothing there. Then, you go again and *Wowie Zip*, which are a couple of words we got in The Gang that mean Impossible and Unbelievable and Absolutely the Greatest, there is something new staring you right in the face! Maybe it's a bird nest or a new bunch of woodpecker holes or even blossoms or leaves. You never know what you might find if you look hard enough. And I sure do look hard enough sometimes. I do!

So you can see why Mom doesn't want another boy, can't you? I mean, she'd have too much to do. All I have to say about it is that I'd give everything I've got to have a brother. I wouldn't hold anything back either. I'll tell you that I'd do anything and everything she ever asked if she got me a brother. No questions asked. I'd just do it.

To tell you the truth, I suppose that I oughta be going back because she's usually cooled down by now and wondering where I am. She always gets that way. You'd think the way she acts that I was going to die. Boy, she really acts strange sometimes, I swear.

Before I go, I never did tell you what the guys in The Gang call me, did I? Well, they call me Mouthpiece. Isn't That Something?

You know, a Mouthpiece — that's what they call a Lawyer, and a Lawyer is supposed to be somebody really smart, and when a Lawyer talks, people listen. I told Murderin' Sam that one time, and he really laughed. He said, "Yeah, you're smart all right." And you know, I guess I really am!

BUDDY NELSON'S HANGAR is as big as man's imagination. There are no locks on the doors and the only membership requirements are Curiosity, Faith, Desire and Determination.

JUNIOR HIGH

I can remember when I was in grade school how sick I was at the thought of Mom, who was pregnant for the second time, getting me a sister. It drove me nuts to think she might have a girl instead of a boy! I desperately wanted a brother, not a sister. What a waste of time that was!

My Father owned and operated a small independent "gyppo" logging company in partnership with Uncle Sandy. (Uncle Alvin had to resign due to a relapse from the malaria that he'd contracted while fighting in the jungles of the Philippines during World War II. Working as a Logger was just physically too hard for Uncle Alvin's body.) Dad worked away from home much of the year. Every time he returned to visit the Family, Mom got pregnant again. By the time I reached the seventh grade in 1952, she was pushing them out

Rock Hill

like rabbits, for heaven's sake! Three brothers in three years. Eventually, a sister would arrive. Every time I looked up, there was a new face at the kitchen table. It seemed like Dad and Mom were trying to have enough children to form their own football team. As for me, I am in the eighth grade; I am growing older and ready for new adventures.

Some of those new adventures are taking place right here at home. Because of my new brothers, Mom badly needs help taking care of the Family and keeping the house clean. Guess who has that job? Right, it is the number-one son, Jim. Mom said she would be absolutely overwhelmed if I didn't help her. Mom told me, "The knowledge about homecare, cooking, and laundry you are getting will become very valuable as you get older — especially to your wife! Whatever girl takes a risk on you as a husband will be getting a partner who knows how to help take care of the home. That is a real asset, Jim. It is ridiculous for men to believe that taking care of children and keeping the house clean is just a woman's responsibility. Many men do feel that way unfortunately." Mom asked my Dad repeatedly about hiring a part-time helper lady. Guess what? Dad hired a lady to help clean the house a few hours weekly. I told Mom, "Isn't Dad great?" She said, "Well, he better do it or he can just keep his brains in his pocket for all I care." Gee, Mom can sure say some funny things sometimes!

Junior High features classes in different rooms taught by different Teachers. The day is much more interesting and passes far quicker than time spent in Elementary School where a student spends all day with one Teacher in one room.

The total seventh and eighth grade class size is roughly fifty students with homeroom classes broken into two groups of twenty-five. My Homeroom Teacher in seventh grade was Mr. Jack Gold, a favorite of the girls because of his looks and personality. The boys considered him a wimp based on his statement that Athletics in school should be eliminated because sports activities interfere with Academics. He taught seventh grade English, Boys' Health, and Mathematics with zeal. Allowing each student only one question per class, he wanted no horseplay, although his demeanor guaranteed plenty of it. More than once, Mr. George Jinks, the Rock Hill High School Assistant Football Coach, who taught boys' Junior High Physical Education, entered the classroom to instill discipline: "You guys sit down and shut up or you'll be invited down to the gym for calisthenics thirty minutes straight." Mr. Gold always resented Mr. Jinks's interference but never said a word when Jinks said, "Holy cow, Gold, are you running a classroom or a pool hall?"

Mrs. Alice Bore, a red-haired woman whose youthful beauty had flown away after years of marriage to a Pentecostal Minister, was the other seventh grade Homeroom Teacher. The Parson didn't allow his flock, let alone his wife, to wear make-up or dress in a manner that would attract attention. She taught seventh grade English, Science, and Literature and liked the boys better than the girls. Mrs. Bore was constantly on the look out for the girl who swished her dress a little too loud when she turned a corner or the chance to catch someone red-handed passing a note to another student, boy

Rock Hill

or girl. A famous saying of hers was "Let's keep our eyes on the ball, and let's mind our P's and Q's so our X, Y, and Z's don't run over us." Classmate Willie Jaywood, a short student who must have weighed all of seventy-five pounds, was blessed with crossed eyes that at times made all the guys wonder in what direction he was looking. We figured his eyes were crossed from spending too much time watching his P's and Q's. My good friend, and an old member of The Gang, Classmate Terry Bones, said that while Jaywood was watching Mrs. Bore's ball, his X, Y' and Z's ran over his head.

A great story about Mrs. Bore was told by my special friend and Classmate Jane White, immediately after the incident happened. During girls' seventh grade Health Class, Mrs. Bore was standing at the front of the room reading material from a Health textbook. Suddenly, the elastic waistband on her panties lost tension, causing the panties to fall to her ankles. Without missing a word in the text, the Teacher looked down, stepped out of the leg holes of her bloomers, picked them up, and with a flourish, put the panties into a jacket pocket. Nary a word did she comment. Jane White said the incident proved why a woman was better off not wearing panties!

Last week Sam Wilcox, also a member of my old gang, made news in Mrs. Bore's class. Sam was caught with a girl's make-up mirror attached to the top of one boot, sliding the mirror underneath a girl's dress. Mrs. Bore immediately ordered Sam to the Principal's office for discipline It did not take long for Mr. Don and "Big Thunder" to apply a learning lesson that we all thought could be heard throughout Rock Hill, let alone the entire school. Funny thing, though, not once has any of us ever seen or heard Sam Wilcox cry. He is sure one tough guy! Sam told us later that his Dad says, "If you are going to do the crime, you have to be willing to do the time."

Sam also told us that he did it so he could see the girl's "Love Muffin." Sam said he noticed a few girls who had a sly smile on their face when he did it! Bones asked Sam if any of the girls had forgotten their panties. Sam replied, "Since I am a gentleman, it is a precious secret known only to me! Besides, I don't want to get into any more trouble by getting you young boys too excited!"

Mr. Jack Gold's claim to fame during the year was causing an uproar over Selma Louis. Selma had told her Dad, a long-haul truck driver, that Mr. Gold put his hand on her "Love Spot." We guys thought that was a stretch because the girl weighed over two hundred and fifty pounds and we doubted if just one hand was big enough. Anyway, the Principal, School Superintendent, and even the School Board got involved to douse the flames of controversy. Mr. Louis threatened to horsewhip Mr. Gold if he ever touched Selma again. Mr. Gold maintained it was a complete fabrication by a lonely child and offered to take a lie-detector test. In the end, Selma was transferred to the other homeroom where Mrs. Bore made it crystal clear such creative foolishness would not be tolerated. Though the tempest was soon over, it was not quickly forgotten. We guys always believed Mr. Gold was guilty of some mischief and still thought he eyed the girls a little too much. After all, he wasn't above praising the girls with touching gestures, which most girls seemed to like. It's funny, though, Jane White couldn't stand Mr. Gold. She said he gave her the creeps because he acted like he could see through her clothing. Bones said, "What clothing?" Jane laughed and told Bones, "Wouldn't you really like to know for sure."

Seventh grade was when the guys began to notice the girls were starting to fill out in certain places. Their chests were getting bigger. They were starting to wear lipstick, perfume, and stretch-waist belts that made their boobs stick out even more. Every girl, it seemed, was always running a brush through her hair. Girls were taking a little more time in the lavatory and looked better coming out than when they entered. Additionally, the girls were starting to notice the boys a lot more.

Couples began to pair up. Hands were being held, boys were walking girls to the lunchroom and the bus. Birthday parties were being planned. Health Class suddenly took on a more important role in our lives. We hung on every word until Mr. Gold - The Hypocrite, said, "When I was your age, girls were only pictures in a book. We should now, and always, keep our thoughts pure and our hands free from sin." When the bell rang at the end of class, Sam Wilcox hollered, "Oh sure, listen to Preacher Gold, won't you? Better ask Selma Louis about that advice." Mr. Gold glared at Sam Wilcox as we all jumped up to exit the classroom. Sam though, glared right back with not a word said between the two.

JUNIOR HIGH

PE is, of course, the favorite class of the day for the boys. In the fall, we play eighth grade touch football and always have a boxing glove grudge match or two caused by some guy "touching" another guy a little too hard. Usually, after the hard feelings are resolved, the game and friendship is renewed. In the winter, we play basketball and dodge ball. Once again an occasional boxing match ensues when someone gets hit in the head at close range with the ball. It is against the rule to aim above the shoulders, but more than one fistfight has started when the rule is purposely ignored.

In the spring, there is no Junior High School Baseball League. "Work Up" Baseball is the main sport: As a batter either strikes out, or is "put out," he moves to the end of the order—Right Field. With each new out, he moves from Right Field to Center Field to Left Field to Third Base, etc. Thus, a Player gets to experience playing at every position. At the same time throughout the entire year, Mr. George Jinks, who teaches Junior High PE, practically wears us out with calisthenics: push-ups, side-straddle hops, leg-ups, sit-ups, and chin-ups on the bars. It is always funny watching some of the guys who are not athletically inclined trying to accomplish some of the drills. Mr. Jinks overlooks a lack of natural ability but is really hard on the athletic guys who slack. He is also willing to overlook a lack of skill and coordination, but woe to the ones who do not try. The athletes who shirk are the ones who really feel Jinks' verbal lash without mercy. If a guy has athletic talent, Mr. Jinks expects you to play at or above your potential. "Men," he says, "be proud you have a pair. Don't act like a

Rock Hill

bunch of pussywillows. When I tell you to move, don't ask to where, just take action. Put your brain in neutral and muscles in drive. This isn't math class, you know. I expect all of you to get in shape and stay there." Two-hundred-pound five-foot-one-inch John Davis laughs when he hears that statement. John always says, "I was born to be a manager, not a player."

Now that we are in the eighth grade, we act like we are "lords of the manor," first without equals. It is the last year of being high and mighty before becoming peons again as lowly Rock Hill High School Freshman.

My Homeroom Teacher is Mrs. Louise Stride, a tall gaunt-looking woman who has taught for over thirty years. She says her first school was a one-room rural schoolhouse in Nebraska with only seven students representing seven different grades. She has absolutely no sense of humor and tolerates no talking in class. She has a furious glare that can slice an iron skillet in half. More than one guy has felt the rap of her ruler on an uncovered arm or knuckle for being a "smart aleck."

While Mrs. Stride is hard on the boys, she is even more demanding with the girls. Always pushing higher education for girls, she once or twice a week exclaims, "You don't have to be just a breed sow, ladies." In response, the guys always yell in unison, "Why not?" much to her dismay. We know there is safety in numbers, but Lord have mercy if a guy ever gets caught broadcasting solo. To instill class discipline, Mrs. Stride has a surefire threat for those who are creative and can write. It is the dreaded five –hundred - word theme about "The Meaning of Respect and Courtesy." For the slower student, it is always having to print five hundred times "Life Does Not Pay Big Wages To A Smart Aleck." Surprisingly, Sam Wilcox acts pretty good in her class. The rest of us guys think it is the result of previous meetings with Mr. Don, the Principal, and "Big Thunder."

Another surprise is how Jane White and Mrs. Stride get along and respect one another. Jane says Mrs. Stride is a very smart woman who can teach a lot of men a few things. Likewise in front of the class, Mrs. Stride has told Jane on more than one occasion that Jane can accomplish very high goals in her life. Jane just needs to learn her brains and charm should be channeled, not dispensed willy-nilly on any worthless man who happens to strut by. Mrs. Stride says she hopes one day Jane will use her obvious beauty and brains to create a career instead of a reputation.

Mrs. Stride teaches Literature and English. During her Chadron State College years, she says she met Willa Cather, Mari Sandoz, and Amelia Earhart. According to her, all three women stood for what is magnificent and good about the so-called weaker sex: intelligence, creativity, and courage. She says if women ever get their hands on the reins of political power in America, the world, including Rock Hill, will be a better place. We guys start moaning and acting like we are all playing tunes of woe on a violin until the infamous Stride glare halts the symphony.

Today, Louise Stride is very proud of her sex, profession, and family. In her 30's she wed a Nebraska dry land farm boy who had witnessed one too many crop failures during his youth. After service in the US Army during World War I, future husband Stanley Stride came home to marry the old-maid school marm, eventually moving his Family west to better financial times in

Washington State. Stan worked at a plywood mill; Louise raised her four children while teaching school. Stan is an Elk Hunter and a Steelhead Salmon Fisherman; Louise is the intellectual in the Family. One Stride boy, a Graduate of the University of Washington with a Master's Degree in Economics from the University of Chicago, is employed by the Department of Agriculture in Washington, DC. Two daughters are both students at Central Washington State Teachers College, and Mrs. Stride always beams when she talks about them. However, the last child is Dan, a boy always in trouble with the law for underage drinking and poaching deer out of season. Mrs. Stride loves Dan as much as either of her daughters and her oldest son, but always says there is too much of her husband Stan in her son Dan and not enough of her.

We read and write reports on the stories and books she assigns. I must say Mrs. Stride is a demanding but fair teacher. She says her job is to teach us how to read, comprehend, and write. She also says, "If one can read it, one should also be able to understand the content well enough to write about its meaning." Louise Stride is a challenging Teacher who always emphasizes that learning requires intellectual effort and hard work. "When knowledge is the end result," she says, "it will lead to positive action in one's life." We are to realize "the purpose of Literature and the English language is to shed light on man, to enable one to understand his state in life and, perhaps, using the words of others as a catalyst, work for the betterment of mankind." She hopes some of us one day can make our mark in life through writing to add to mankind's knowledge and wisdom.

One day Mrs. Stride gave us a lecture on her early days of teaching in Northwestern Nebraska during the early 1920s. She said she started teaching when she was only nineteen years old with a two-year degree from Chadron State Normal School in Chadron, Nebraska. Her first classroom was a one-room schoolhouse near Crawford, Nebraska. This teaching assignment was one of the most challenging positions she'd had during her long teaching career. She told us there was nothing better than being young and filled with energy and enthusiasm to make the assignment worthwhile. She said at Christmas she still gets cards from a few of her first students.

FORT ROBINSON, c. 1878-1879. An unknown photographer captured one of the last glimpses of Fort Robinson as a frontier garrison, just before construction began to expand the post. Nestled below the buttes near the head of the White River, Fort Robinson was considered by many visitors to be in one of the most scenic spots in the West. (Nebraska State Historical Society, RG151999.

Rock Hill

MOCK CHARGE. With his saber drawn, an officer rides at the head of Troop I 10th Cavalry during a practice charge across the parade grounds at Fort Robinson. (Nebraska State Historical Society, RG1517:93-12.)

Mrs. Stride said she especially liked the area in which she lived and taught. The Northwestern Nebraska Sand hills region was known for its cattle ranches and dry land Farmers. This land was most historic, the home of Fort Robinson which was one of the few early US Army Forts built during the frontier days that remained active through World War II. The Red Cloud Indian Agency was located nearby. The Post was also where the famous 9th and 10th Cavalry were stationed, the Buffalo Soldiers, the All-Black Horse Soldiers of the US Army. Most Americans have no idea how important the Black Troopers were in fighting American Indians to make the West safe for settlement.

During the 1880s, First Sergeant Emanuel Stance of Troop F, 9th Cavalry, the First Black Soldier to win the Congressional Medal of Honor after the Civil War, was stationed at Fort Robinson. He was from Carroll Parish, Lake Providence, Louisiana and joined the US Army in 1867 at the age of 19. After Basic Training in San Antonio, Texas, First Sergeant Emanuel Stance spent 19 years (Yes, that's right 19 years) leading his men, while fighting some of the most ferocious warriors the American Military has ever faced: The Comanche, Kiowa, Kickapoo, Apache, Cheyenne, and Sioux Indians. Unfortunately, near the end of his US Army 20 year Career, he was murdered outside of Fort Robinson, the killers never caught, prosecuted or punished. It is a terrible chapter in the Annals of otherwise Magnificent US Army Military History. Mrs. Stride said, if First Sergeant Emanuel Stance had been a White man, the Authorities would have gone to the ends of the earth to catch the killer. And, if the killer had been a Black man, he would have undoubtedly been hung. (Thank God, America is a better Country today.) She also said that First Sergeant Emanuel Stance was now buried at Ft. McPherson National Cemetery along the Oregon Trail, just East of North Platte, Nebraska; and that perhaps someday he would be properly honored for his service to his Country by being laid to rest at Arlington National Cemetery with the rest of Americas Military War Heroes.

Rock Hill

Chief Red Cloud

RED CLOUD (MAHPIYA LUTA, c. 1822-1909). Probably the best- known Oglala leader, Red Cloud was headman of the Itesica, or Bad Face Band, but his influence extended beyond his immediate camp. Red Cloud, shown here in 1877, was often viewed as the primary spokesman for all of the Oglala at the agency that bore his name. (Photograph by D. S. Mitchell; Smithsonian Institution, NAA 00210800.)

The great Sioux War Chief Crazy Horse was imprisoned at Fort Robinson and later accidently killed there when he resisted imprisonment. During the 1920s, Fort Robinson was named a Horse Remount Headquarters where horses were bred, raised, and trained for the US Army Calvary. Likewise, the US Army Olympic Equestrian and Polo Teams were periodically stationed there. Finally, during World War II, a US Army K-9 Company trained guard and bomb-sniffing dogs for use all over the world;

plus, many POWs from Europe were kept at Fort Robinson. These German and Italian prisoners helped farmers and ranchers all over the Upper Midwest plant and harvest their crops, when manpower needs were urgent because our own men were fighting overseas.

Mrs. Stride advised us to always be on the lookout during our travels to visit old military posts and National and State Parks of historical interest. "There is nothing better than actually seeing the famous places that we have read about in our History books. It is unfortunate, but all too many people do not take the time to see where our Ancestors worked, lived, fought our Country's battles and died to give us the great United States of America. When given the opportunity, many people are just either too busy or too lazy for their own good. An "On Site Historical Tour" missed is an education lost. We must never forget that truth."

Much to our surprise, Mrs. Louise Stride, with a big smile on her otherwise dour face, closed her talk by telling us that she remembered when she was "The Belle Of The Ball" at many US Army Fort Robinson Holiday Dances that the Officers held at the Post. She surprised us all by stating that she could have married many times during that period if she had wanted to give up her teaching career. Apparently, most rural school districts would not allow a Teacher to teach after marriage. For Mrs. Stride, being her own boss was far better than having some handsome, young "West Point Whippersnapper" order her around for the rest of her life. She also said that because Horsemanship was still very important in the US Army at that time, especially with the US Army Olympic Equestrian and Polo Teams headquartered at

Fort Robinson, her free time was always filled with horseback rides with some very dashing US Army Officers. The girls in the class thought that news was interesting. We guys also thought that Mrs. Stride probably could have shared some interesting tales about "Pitching A Little Woo", too. Such stories, unfortunately, were not forthcoming!

Franklin Heber is the other eighth grade Homeroom Teacher. Mr. "Hebe," as he likes to be called, is about five foot seven and weighs two hundred and eighty pounds. He has a big smile for everyone and an even bigger laugh if something happens in class that is truly funny. His forte is Science and Mathematics, two subjects I mostly endure. Mr. Hebe is an "equal opportunity" Teacher. He plays no favorites. Patiently he waits for the student who has difficulty subtracting 1/8 from ¼ or understanding what H_2O means. Mr. Hebe says it took him five years to get through a four-year college. He says that he understands that, "school can be hard at times. It sure was for me." We all laugh and like him for saying it. Mrs. Stride says that part about College is not true because Mr. Hebe is a member of The Phi Beta Kappa Society. Mrs. Stride says this is quite an honor which is given to only outstanding students with very high grades. His "Certificate of Membership" is prominently displayed on a wall in his classroom.

In class, Mr. Hebe wears both a belt and suspenders. He says it is his conservative Southern Baptist roots showing through. He always dresses in a dark suit, a white shirt, and a black bow tie. His red hair is parted in the middle and his voice is "The Sound of Thor"! The first time he gave instructions in class, the guys

JUNIOR HIGH

RED POLO TEAM CHAMPION. Shown on horseback, from left to right, are T/4 Rising, Captain Powers, Captain Hill, Staff Sergeant Jones. (Nebraska State Historical Society, RG1517-45-27.)

U.S. ARMY OLYMPIC EQUESTRIAN TEAM TRAINING. In June 1935, the army's equestrian team arrived to train for the summer at Fort Robinson. This photograph was taken in August during one of the team's public exhibitions. (Nebraska State Historical Society, RG1517-49-2.)

were astonished at his vocal volume. To maintain discipline or teach a certain point he will always shout you into your proper place. Franklin Heber is a bachelor with a pet Chihuahua for a child. He says a dog isn't likely to nag him into any objectionable activity like dumping garbage when he doesn't feel like it or losing weight because it is hard on your heart. He says next to his well-marbled steaks, he likes his freedom even more.

⌘ ⌘ ⌘

For the boys who love athletics, Mr. Don, the Principal, is our favorite. In the fall he organizes afterschool touch football games. He positions the players and devises the plays. He also guides the quarterbacks to facilitate play calling. He shows the bigger guys how to block, the tall fellows how to play end, and the backs how to carry and run with the ball. Along with two other guys, I play quarterback under Mr. Don's direction. Everyone loves playing defense, even if it is just touch. Mr. Don says, "In High School, because you boys are by nature very aggressive on defense, tackling will come easy for you."

In the winter we play basketball in a Junior High League with four nearby schools. Mr. Don played guard on a College team and is our Coach. He says our group has four years of tremendous basketball success ahead of us in Rock Hill High School. We have great young talent and if we work hard for four years, by our senior year we could win the Washington State Class B Title. Team effort is the key. The boys who play together generally win; the guys who play just for themselves lose. Success on the field of sports is like the real world: Teamwork pays big dividends. He always emphasizes that organized effort has a better chance of succeeding than one person trying to be a hero. Mr. Don was a Commander on a US Navy Destroyer during World War II in the South Pacific. His favorite saying is "It takes a crew to run a ship; the Captain just gives the orders." He is always telling anyone who will listen, "The boys of that class are going a long way on the 'street of success' in sports and life. They will be a class who will make their Teachers, Coaches, Parents, and the town of Rock Hill proud."

Hey, guess what the guys and I did on Sunday? We went to Chehalis for a Harlem Globetrotters game! Mom drove us to Chehalis where we saw the Globetrotters play the Washington Nationals. What a game to watch! Boy, watching the Globetrotter Star - Reece "Goose" Tatum, "The Clown Prince of Basketball," handle a basketball was absolutely fantastic! Gee, was that fellow one of the most outstanding basketball players I have ever seen! It was unbelievable how long his arms were and how good he was!

After the game we were able to talk with the Coach of the Harlem Globetrotters and the Washington Nationals. Boy, was he a super guy! His name was Mr. Elmer H. Ripley. He was one of the kindest fellows I ever met. The guys and I told him about our Rock Hill Junior High team. His reaction was like he really cared about our team. We could tell his interest in us by his questions of how we practiced and played our games.

It was easy to see he was a very successful coach who knew a great deal about coaching basketball. Coach Ripley said that as long as we always played together as a team and practiced all elements of our game we would have great success.

Believe it or not, on Tuesday I received a postcard inviting me to attend a Thursday night Globetrotters game to sit on the player's bench with the team, WOW! Mom said, "No, it is a school night and you cannot miss your sleep." I tried to tell Mom how important this was to me, I didn't like her telling me I couldn't go! But when Mom puts her foot down, I know there's little chance of changing her mind. I did ask Dad what he thought and would he try to get Mom to reconsider? He said, "No, Mom is the boss. Do you want to get me into trouble with your Mother? I am sorry Jim; No, I will not!" So that was that: I didn't get to sit on the Globetrotters bench, dog-gone-it!

The next week, I received a very nice letter from Coach Ripley. He asked me to meet the team at other locations while the Globetrotters were traveling in the Pacific Northwest. Unfortunately, the cities where the games were played were too far away from Rock Hill. Dad and Mom said Coach Ripley was very kind to write me. Coach Ripley is obviously a great Coach and a very friendly person who cares deeply about the game of Basketball and the players who play the game. Much to my surprise, Coach Ripley sent me a really outstanding book about Basketball: *Basketball for the Player, the Fan and The Coach* by Arnold "Red" Auerbach, Head Coach of the Boston Celtics. Isn't that something!

JUNIOR HIGH

Everyone in Rock Hill knows that Dad and Mr. Don are very good friends. Once, Dad shared his thoughts about Mr. Don with me. Dad believes that whatever success I have achieved in school to date is due in large part because of the outstanding role Mr. Don performs as the Principal of Rock Hill's Elementary and Junior High School. He says it is no easy task to manage so many talented Professional Teachers at one time. Mr. Don's ability to inspire his staff with his skills of discipline and organization is remarkable. Dad said, **"Education is the key to developing America's future citizens and is the foundation of our way of life. Teachers are the men and women who must provide young people with the information they need to know about our past and present and to prepare for the future.**

"Indeed, Teachers have the most meaningful and challenging career in all of Rock Hill. Unfortunately today, Teachers are underpaid, over worked, and unappreciated by many." Dad added, "Your Elementary and Junior High years are very important, Jim, for your success in High School and College will depend a great deal on the educational foundation you build during these early years. You must work hard and pay attention in class." In conclusion, Dad said, "I am pleased that Mr. Don has a number of male Teachers on his staff. It is very worthwhile to have a male's point of view at all grade levels to help develop boys into men. Female Teachers are outstanding at teaching boys as well as girls to read, write, and do math, but a large part of a boy's growth in

Elementary and Junior High School is learning how to think and act as a man." Men, in his opinion, have an edge over women in that task.

While Dad and I were talking, Mom was listening to our conversation without comment. Pretty soon, she said to Dad, "Jupe, I do not agree with you. Women Teachers are just as capable as any man when it comes to turning boys into men. A woman's love, understanding, and encouragement will help a boy overcome the challenges he faces in becoming a man. Your own son, Jim, is a fine example of a woman's ability to mold a boy into a man. Granted, he still has a lot to learn in the future, but I believe female Teachers will definitely play an important role in his mental and physical development. I say thank God for that fact. Just remember the impact Miss Heart had on Jim in the fifth grade. When he was sick and missed two months of the school year, it was Miss Heart who encouraged him to persevere to get well in spite of his illness that could have killed him. As I told you before, if our son had been older, Jim would have wanted to marry her, for heaven's sake! Miss Heart and I laughed many times about his puppy love for her. She was a godsend, believe me. Now just look at your son; All the Teachers say he is smart, hardworking, and an absolutely outstanding athlete for his age, size, and health history."

Dad replied, "Daisy, all the same. in my opinion, men make the best mentors for boys learning how to grow into manhood."

When Mom mentioned Miss Heart, it brought back a beautiful memory; I think about her even today more than I wish to admit. Boy, what a gorgeous woman she was! She had blonde hair, blue eyes, warm ivory-white skin, and a figure that would stop an Aviator's Wristwatch. And smart, why, Miss Heart was one of the most intelligent people I have ever known! When I asked her a question, she always had a correct answer. One time I did ask Mr. Don whatever happened to Miss Heart after she left Rock Hill School. He said, "Oh Jim, the beautiful, single Teachers all run off to find their Sir Galahad. In Miss Heart's case, she married a giant of a man named Mr. Al Green. I guess he was a jolly fellow with lots of money and they have three very gifted children in the Midwest somewhere who make their Parents extremely proud." To Mr. Don I said, "I was happy God had blessed her with such Treasure." But to myself I said, "Though I was not to be the lucky Pilot to fly Miss Heart to the altar, I have no complaints! Miss Charlotte Heart gave me the greatest Gift of all: Beautiful Memories To Help Handle The Challenges Of Life. Though I May Never See Her Again, My Memory Of Her Will Always Live In My Mind."

⌘ ⌘ ⌘

One class that every guy enjoys is eighth grade Woodshop. We are separate from our homeroom environment and learning a trade. The Teacher, new to the District, is always comparing our class to those he had elsewhere: "Last year where

I taught, my students were very conscientious while you boys seem to think Woodshop is just a game." Most students respond with a groan while Boomer Jones starts complaining he is confused about the difference between *nomenclature* and *use*, recalling another phrase the teacher likes to use: "It's amazing to me how some of you boys don't know the difference between nomenclature and use. I swear that some of you don't even know the difference between a jigsaw and a T-square, let alone their use!

The Teacher's name is Mr. Horace P. Birdwinkle, which is enough in itself to make any warm-blooded eighth grade boy break into a snicker. He is six foot five inches tall weighing all of 160 pounds. He wears a brown shop gown constantly and has huge thick eyeglasses that look like the lenses have been made from the bottoms of glass fruit jars. He is rumored to smoke a corncob pipe in the nearby boiler room but we can never catch him savoring his Prince Albert smoking tobacco, kept in its tin container in his right top desk drawer.

In the eighth grade, Woodshop class is an hour long, which is usually spent half in the classroom, half in the equipment room. We are first taught the names of the tools and their use; then, Mr. Birdwinkle demonstrates methods of operation whereupon the class will relocate to the shop room to actually use the equipment. Before leaving the classroom, there is always the standard warning: "Remember, gentlemen, safety always pays. It's easy to lose fingers or other appendages." Mr. Birdwinkle then smiles. "Please be careful. I was not placed on this earth to teach immature idiots how to cut off fingers - your own or your tool partner's."

We each have a classmate tool partner for safety reasons. In reality there isn't much chance of doing harm to ourselves or anyone else since eighth grade boys are not allowed to use the power equipment. Our wooden works of art are all created using handsaws, planes, and sanders. All painting is done by hand as well. Mr. Birdwinkle tolerates absolutely no horseplay in the shop room. If caught flipping paint on a classmate or using the tools in an unsafe manner, the student caught in the act is ordered back to the classroom and a remedial lesson is quickly taught. Believe me, Mr. Birdwinkle is not a Teacher who waits for someone else to administer his discipline. He is very quick to use one of three paddles that hang on wall hooks just behind his desk. The names of the paddles are Larry, Moe, and Curly, Mr. Birdwinkle's favorite Hollywood movie stars. The student nominated for the remedial lesson of proper classroom behavior gets to pick the instrument of his instruction. Horace Phillip Birdwinkle always orally underscores the swing of the "attitude adjuster" with the fact that "the shop is a dangerous place where one plus one must never equal three. Common sense must prevail at all times. If some idiot makes a mistake, you or someone else could be maimed for life."

The main project in eighth grade Woodshop is a kitchen cutting board approximately twelve inches by twelve inches, one inch thick, perfectly square. Most of the time is spent learning the names of the tools, how to use the tools, what tools to use for various jobs, and proper tool care. If it weren't for the horsing around that a student can get away with in the classroom (but absolutely not in the equipment room), the hour would be quite boring. Most guys who really like to make things use their Dad's power equipment at home. When pressed to explain the school policy, Mr. Birdwinkle maintains the school's liability insurance restricts eighth graders to hand tools (or hand *fools* as we call them).

In the classroom, jokes and wisecracks are always part of the banter that passes between student and Teacher. When students go from their seats to watch a demonstration, some student will surely goose another. As long as the activity doesn't distract from the "learning environment," Mr. Birdwinkle will tolerate a bit of friendly noise (Horseplay!) Go too far, though, and an "attitude adjustment" will commence with "one of the Three Stooges swatting somebody's brains." as Mr. Birdwinkle says.

One memorable event in Woodshop was the day I saw my first sex book. Brian Sharp, one of the older guys in the class who's from a Logging Family, was the Librarian. I was knee-deep in dead brain cells trying to get my kitchen cutting board exactly square when I noticed a commotion over by the shop area where the brooms were kept. Guys were laughing and holding their stomachs. It was obviously pretty good. I immediately ceased the work I was doing on my masterpiece to find out what was so funny.

After walking over to the group and asking what was going on, I was given a small booklet about 2½ inches by 3 inches in size. It was a black and white comic book featuring Popeye and Olive Oyl. Holy cow, I couldn't believe it. Popeye had a hammer that was about fourteen inches long and Olive Oyl was doing everything but ignoring it. I'll tell you she was doing things to Popeye's hammer that even an oversexed eighth-grade boy couldn't imagine. I had never seen anything like this classic and neither had the other guys. We tried to get Brian to loan it to us so we could make copies but to no avail. I guess an older brother in the US Army had given the comic book to him when the brother was home on leave. Brian said it was a special gift. We all agreed. Even Sam Wilcox offered Brian two dollars for the booklet, but Brian said no. He wanted to savor its contents a bit longer. He also said he knew a few girls who might enjoy such humor, which the rest of us thought sounded interesting. The comic book was soon put away though because everyone knew if Mr. Birdwinkle caught a student with such a sample of "outhouse" humor, more than a simple "attitude adjustment" would be forthcoming.

One story about Mr. Birdwinkle that circulated throughout the school concerned a couple of Rock Hill High School students named David Elgin and Steven Zander. Both guys were known for their classroom antics, and one particular week they had been having an ongoing farting contest. The night before the famous conclusion Steven had slept at David's house. The two contestants had binged themselves with mustard and pork and bean sandwiches. Then they came to school the next day prepared to have a final fart off. The contest peaked in

Mr. Birdwinkle's High School Woodshop Class: The smell lay terrible and heavy in the air.

It just so happened that on this particular day, a Paint Salesman was visiting the Woodshop. Mr. Birdwinkle was showing the guest his facilities. Upon walking into the shop room, the two men encountered the stink. Without missing a step, Mr. Birdwinkle turned to the Salesman to say, "Hmm, smells like the boys have been running the sander over the paint again." The Salesman never said a word but was last seen vigorously rubbing his nose and wiping a tear out of his eye!

While I enjoy the general information we learn in Woodshop, I know being a Carpenter is not the best career choice for me. Other guys thrive on making things, but I really can never "catch the thrill of creating something with your hands," as Mr. Birdwinkle describes the feeling. As far as equipment, I want it to be an airplane. My goal is to be a Pilot not a Carpenter. Because Woodshop and Horace P. Birdwinkle do teach the lessons of safe tool operation and respect for common sense, I realize serious harm can result from sloppy or haphazard use of any piece of equipment. Dad said, **"In life, where risk is ever present, a person must always exercise caution and care to prevent foolish loss of life or limb. It makes no difference, Jim, if you are operating a handsaw or a power saw, a lawn mower or a Caterpillar D-8 Cat, a Skagit diesel-engine-powered Logging Donkey or a Douglas DC-3 Airliner, it is absolutely imperative that you always think through the task ahead of you before you act. Any machine or piece of equipment is only**

as safe or capable as the man responsible for its operation. If you gain nothing but this fact from one year of Woodshop, it is a lesson worth keeping for a lifetime."

⌘ ⌘ ⌘

My favorite fun class is Junior High Band, a true high note. Every student who is musically inclined participates; the problem is, so do some who are not. The Rock Hill Junior High and High School Band Leader, Mr. Jack Amburger, tries his best to allow each student the musical instrument of his choice. Occasionally, however, even his wonderful personality is tested. Mr. Ambuger, affectionately known as "Ham" to all students, is challenged by boys who want to play drum solos in the style of Gene Krupa or coronet players who think loud trumpet runs are needed in the middle of a band rendition of *"America The Beautiful."*

Our musical education started in the sixth grade. During the first days of the new school year there was much debate about what instrument to play. Ham encouraged every student to make his own choice. Students soon learned that holding the correct lip position to sound the right trumpet note was not easy. In the beginning, many boys thought the ability to play trumpet like Harry James would some day surely lead to winning the heart of their own special Betty Grable lookalike. In time however, more than a few switched to the less demanding woodwind family or to the loud drum brigade where some guys took great pride in breaking the eardrums

Rock Hill

of their fellow musicians with a run or two of glorious, deafening paradiddles!

For most students, playing in the Band is an important step in the school ladder of social and educational progress. Students are told by Teachers and Parents that music is an important part of a well - rounded education. Mom says, "Music is food for the Soul and the ability to play a musical instrument can be a gift of great joy and personal satisfaction." I selected the clarinet to learn to play because I always liked the sound of "The Licorice Stick." Being able to sit next to Jane White who also plays the clarinet clinched the decision! When I first began to practice at home, my Dad was quick to point out that I would surely become the Lewis County Squawk/Squeak King. I said, "Dad, just give me time and I will make you proud of my musical talent." Dad laughed and said, "Time and my poor ears will tell!"

Students also know an hour spent in Band is an hour away from English, Science, or Mathematics classes. Sometimes the hour can also be used to complete overdue homework if necessary, though Ham is not always pleased when other class work intervenes. However, because he depends on the goodwill of fellow Teachers to excuse band students for extra practice just prior to concerts, Ham overlooks the occasional student working on other class assignments.

Boys especially like Band because it is a chance to sit close to the girls. More than one heart-thumping crush has been started during band practice. There is always an opportunity to move a chair for a girl, arrange the music stand just so, touch a girl on the arm, or even better, "accidentally" brush your leg against her. At Band practice young love is certainly in the air, along with every sound known to man that can be launched from a musical instrument.

In the fall, once students have regained their musical expertise dormant over the summer, song selection centers on marching songs that can be played on Friday nights at Rock Hill High School Football Games to encourage the crowd to support the team. Songs like *"On Wisconsin,"* the Notre Dame fight song, and John Phillip Sousa's *"Stars and Stripes Forever"* are special favorites. Since many of the Rock Hill High School Band members play on the athletic teams, there are always openings for accomplished Junior High players to assist the High School Band. The eighth grade girls especially enjoy this opportunity because "Pep Band" allows them to associate with older boys. The guys don't mind helping out because, one, the band members get in free to the games and, two, a seat is also guaranteed on the "Rooter" bus for games away from home. For Junior High students, who are too young to have a driver's license or own a used car, this is a real plus.

The school provides the large horns like the tubas, trombones, French horns, saxophones, and drums both bass and snare. The woodwind instruments like the clarinet and flute are rented or purchased from a music store in Chehalis, the county seat thirty miles west of Rock Hill. Parents who purchase instruments are always guaranteed by the music store to either buy them back at the end of the school year, or

Rock Hill

immediately, if plans change. Poor Families whose children have real musical talent have instruments provided by either the community service clubs or wealthy townspeople. Mr. Amburger knows who the truly needy and talented are and never fails to find financial supporters for the Rock Hill School Band Program. He can spot musical talent a mile away and is a genius at filling up his band classes because his love of music and life affects everyone. More than one student began a lifetime appreciation of music in Junior High Band thanks to Mr. Amburger's enthusiasm and encouragement..

One of the biggest events of the year is the Christmas concert which takes place during December, just prior to vacation. After Thanksgiving, band practice features religious songs as well as songs of the season. *"O Little Town of Bethlehem," "Silent Night," "We Three Kings," "White Christmas," "Rudolph the Red-Nosed Reindeer," and "Frosty the Snowman"* are all favorites. The Junior High Band usually plays the opening portion of the concert. The Rock Hill High School Boys and Girls Chorus and both the Junior High and the High School Bands complete the program. There are also featured soloists: piano and vocal. A previous vocal soloist was rumored to have left Rock Hill upon graduation to sing with a famous touring dance band. Some of the older High School boys who knew her said the girl could sing better laying down than she could standing up. Apparently, the bandleader liked the sound of her "horizontal voice" the best. Only thing, no one could ever name the singer. When asked if the story was true, Mr. Amburger just smiled and said, "Yes, I have heard that one, too."

Mr. Jack Amburger is a terrific person. He is the friendliest Teacher I ever had. A smile always excuses even the worst notes of struggling musicians. I especially like him because he was raised in Montana and was a Radio Operator on a US Army Douglas C-47 in the South Pacific during World War II. The Amburgers, who are of the Catholic Faith, had four daughters in a row until their son, Randy, finally arrived. The townspeople showered the family with presents and joy at the occasion. One guy said old Ham would have wound up without a place at the table, if that boy hadn't arrived.

To earn extra money to raise his large Family, Mr. Amburger plays piano in a large dance band that entertains at a fancy hotel in Longview on Saturday nights. He is an outstanding pianist. There is no doubt Mr. Amburger could have made his living with a nationally known band or orchestra if he had wanted to travel. Instead, he devoted his life to Music Education and his beautiful Family.

Winter months for the band feature seasonal selections and fight songs to support the Rock Hill High School Basketball Team. Games are held on Tuesday and Friday nights. Because the basketball team requires fewer players, fewer substitute Junior High Band members are necessary. The gymnasium is small, making the sound of the Band very loud. Too loud, some grumpy townspeople think.

The other musical events of the year are the Spring Fest and the Lewis County Regional Band Concert, which is held in Chehalis at a larger school. By April and May after learning and practicing for almost a full school year, the Junior High Band sounds pretty good. The degree of difficulty of the music has increased and the individual mastery of the instruments has improved. It is amazing, really, how well the band can play. Sure, there is the occasional note off key from somewhere in the group, but all in all, it is an absolute miracle what has been accomplished in a few short months of practice. Some of the better student musicians have even begun thinking of playing music as a part-time occupation to earn extra money. Not me though! I'm afraid an Artie Shaw I will never be! Dad says I better stick to talking for a living. He also says that he hopes he's not destined to be forced to use an ear trumpet when he reaches old age because of my clarinet practice at home! Mom just laughs and tells Dad to "Butt out" and leave her musical prodigy alone!

The Spring Fest is held in late April on a Friday night. Once again the program features the Rock Hill Junior High Band, the High School Boys and Girls Chorus, and the High School Band. Religious songs like "*Give Me That Old-Time Religion*" and "*It's No Secret What God Can Do*," seasonal songs like "*Easter Parade*" and "*Here Comes Peter Cottontail*" and patriotic songs like "*God Bless America*" are featured. A couple of Sousa marches to excite the crowd always concludes the concert. The Lewis County Regional Band Concert is held in May and is considered by students to be a reward for working hard throughout the year. It is an all-day, late-night affair that involves a school-bus ride to Chehalis, the county seat. The Band Members skip regular classes for the day. On the bus, boys can sit with girls but have to mind their manners since a few Band member mothers are along as chaperones. (Vigilantes!)

I'll never forget one very memorable trip: After arriving at Chehalis High School, seven or eight Bands from other schools throughout Lewis County were seated together in the gymnasium. The Band Teachers selected the individual musical pieces each would direct. Then, from 10:00 a.m. until noon the huge group practiced together. At noon, lunch was served in the school cafeteria: hot dogs or hamburgers, French fries, cake, and milk. Practice resumed at 2:00 p.m. and continued until 4:00 p.m. Then everyone took a break for dinner and relaxed until the concert. That night at 7:00 p.m. with three thousand people in attendance, the four-hundred-member mass band played a concert that climaxed with the addition of a world famous guest soloist: Mr. Raphael Mendez, The Classical Trumpet Virtuoso! It was an unforgettable night. Mr. Mendez, one of the world's greatest classic trumpeters and movie-star handsome in a beautiful white tuxedo, blasted the air with his golden horn. It almost made us band members feel like we were playing on a Hollywood sound stage. It was a golden-horned memory guaranteed to last a lifetime.

⌘ ⌘ ⌘

My favorite sport is football, but in Junior High we just play games of touch football among ourselves. There is no

Rock Hill

league. On offense I play quarterback, but my favorite position is linebacker on defense. I plan to tackle someone head on. I may not be very big, but I know I can hit a ball player pretty hard. Mr. Don says, "It's because you are very quick. Weight times speed equals force, which can be deceptive in a small man!"

I told my Dad what Mr. Don had to say about my size. Dad said, **"Jim, I have been wanting to talk to you about your size as well. Now God made you, son, the size you are for a reason. At five foot one inch and less than one hundred pounds, what you lack in height and weight you will have to make up in energy, stamina, and courage. As you age, to stay competitive you will have to be in as good as shape as possible. You must say Absolutely NO to tobacco and alcohol. You must be a testament to clean living. I have admired the courage you exhibit in playing sports. You have learned how to take a hit and give one back. For a man to succeed in competitive sports, he must learn how to overcome fear of failing or getting hurt. That is done with courage. You must create an inner strength that will give you the confidence to know that you are as competitive as anyone else. This strength is created through knowledge, practice and the will to believe in your God given abilities. When you can compete with others who are bigger, stronger, or taller, you will earn the respect of your teammates.**

"Do not be a braggart, do not be a crybaby when the game doesn't go your way, and do not hesitate to come to the aid of someone being picked on by a bully. Bullies are

nothing more than boys who at heart are cowards. Every man should despise a bully. A bully should never be tolerated. They go through life intimidating others with their words or fists. They thrive on fooling those who do not have that inner strength to overcome their fears to protect themselves. I never want you to get into fights foolishly. I do want you to stand your ground when you are in the right. I also want you to stand up for others who cannot defend themselves, if they have done nothing wrong and are being picked on. If you get into trouble at school for fighting, I will back you up one hundred percent as long as you are always standing for what is right. If you live your life with honor, no one will ever call you 'Shorty.'"

Mr. Don occasionally takes time to encourage our class during P.E. He says our group of guys is very athletic: "Because you have played together as a team since the second grade, you boys will do very well in Rock Hill High School Sports." In the winter we have a basketball team that plays other Junior High schools. I play guard on the team. I am a pretty good dribbler and passer, but, like my buddy Bones says, "when it comes to shooting, you can't hit a bull in the butt with a banjo." As a matter of fact, he claims the other team always prays that when I get the ball, I will try to take a shot. Mr. Don says, "Do not think too much about taking shots. You are the playmaker on the team. Your job is to pass the ball to your teammates. You are the guy who makes a play happen. Let other players score the points. Remember, team play is always smart play!"

We have a Cheerleading Squad that leads the classes in yells at the games. My friend Jane White is a part-time Cheerleader. She is a regular on the squad, but Mrs. Martha Cobb, the Advisor and Girls P.E. Teacher, says Jane kicks her legs too high and sometimes does unauthorized cartwheels and refuses to follow most instructions. Jane sits with the squad in the stands but is not allowed to get out on the floor where Mrs. Martha Cobb says Jane always tries to make a "spectacle" of herself. Jane says Mrs. Cobb is just jealous of what Jane calls her "beautiful equipment." She also says Mrs. Cobb is a prude because she doesn't like Jane's red panties that show through her white tights. I told Jane all the guys do, though, and she just beamed!

One of my best friends on the team is Mason Thompson who plays forward. He is already six feet tall and handsome as a movie star. All the girls think he's a real dreamboat. He's also very smart. His Mother works as a clerk at the Rock Hill Drug Store, and his Father owns a dairy farm. They are originally from California and live about ten miles outside of Rock Hill. Mason is also the oldest boy in our class.

One summer I went on a trip with the Thompson family to Southern California for a vacation. We saw Disneyland, Knott's Berry Farms, and the NBC Television Studios, where we watched *The Tennessee Ernie Ford Show* being televised. When the show was over, I shook Ernie's hand as he entered his limousine; boy, was he handsome, and his rich baritone voice just boomed when he asked me, "How are you, young man?" I said, "Fine, and thank you for asking." Gee, was I thrilled! At home, Mom and I listen to Tennessee Ernie's Religious Albums a lot. I love his deep voice, and Mom says his Hymn and Gospel singing always reminds her of going to Church in the Ozarks years ago.

Later, we went to a beach where we swam in the Pacific Ocean. I also met their younger cousin Gloria who gave me a friendship ring and asked that I think of her once in a while. She was really nice. Upon our return home, I found a couple of letters waiting for me from Gloria. Gee, did they smell nice! She said life was "boring" since her cousins and I had returned home. Gosh, maybe someday we'll meet again.

My job on the basketball team is to feed Mason the ball. He is just a fantastic shot with a basketball. Set shots, jump shots, hook shots—it doesn't matter. Mason seldom misses. When it comes to free throws, Mason is an ace. I'll bet it has been three years since he has missed one of those. Mason doesn't go with girls because he says it harms his juices. He says it's enough just to concentrate on school and the basketball rim. I think, though, he does have a favorite girl but just won't admit it. We Guys all think Mason has a Thing for one of the loveliest, smartest girls in our Class, Nancy Cooper. He won't admit it, though, and gets peeved when we tease him about her. I also suspect that, like the rest of us, Mason has dated Mrs. Palmer once in a while, if you know what I mean. Mason is really a very fine person. Mom and Dad said the Thompson Family is one of the finest Families in all of Rock Hill. Mr. Don says Mason is the smartest, most talented student in our class. In Mr. Don's opinion, Mason will succeed at a very high level at whatever he chooses to do in life.

I haven't yanked the crank much in my life, yet. One afternoon, my Mother did catch me in bed with the cover over my head. She asked me, "What are you doing under there?" I said, "Nothing." She asked, "Then why is the bed shaking?" I lied and said, "Pug is with me and he is scratching fleas." (Every boy should have a dog for emergencies like that.) She laughed and told me, "Lying and doing naughty things will make your nose grow longer and other things shorter." I just said, "Some people ought to mind their own business and leave other people alone!"

One time, I asked Mr. Don, "What about me? How successful do you think I will become?" Mr. Don said, "Jim, you have nothing to worry about as long as you work hard to get prepared for whatever life offers you. You are a talker. Your challenge will always be to learn to walk the walk, not just talk. Talking about it and doing it are two different things. In real life, many people talk about doing something, but all too few people actually take the time to get prepared to win in life. Your success, Jim, will come when you learn that your mouth will get you into trouble unless and until you are able to back up your words with results. When you can combine knowledge with experience, action with perseverance, and accomplishment with humility, you will be successful beyond your greatest dreams."

⌘ ⌘ ⌘

JUNIOR HIGH

My favorite Teacher is Mrs. April Downs, the Librarian and History Teacher. The main reasons I like her are her genuine willingness to help students and her overall knowledge of the books and materials in her Library. Mrs. Downs has a special love for American History. She is very good at her job. She listens to questions and takes time to explain things we don't understand. I do think, however, she likes the boys better than she does the girls in our class. At least that is the opinion of the girls, Jane included.

We guys do believe that the girls on the whole are such crybabies about every little thing. Mrs. Downs said one time that no more than one girl at a time could leave the Library to handle personal problems, whatever THEY are. We boys have speculated that it is something silly like a boob strap that has broken or a zipper that has jammed. We hope one day one of us will get lucky and be called upon to give a distressed damsel a hand, but so far such good fortune has not occurred. We always do wonder, though, what the inside of a girl's lavatory looks like. You can bet your last dollar no guy with a pair ever wants to get caught sneaking in to find out. It shall be forever a mystery what lurks within, I suspect! In reality, the lavatory trips are probably nothing more serious than nature calling or boyfriend or homework problems being discussed, which requires a companion or two for consultation. We eighth grade boys, however, have rich imaginative minds when the subject of the opposite sex comes up.

American History, indeed, is Mrs. Downs's favorite subject. She really gets excited about our forefathers and their contribution to the foundation of this nation. She believes every student ought to know why we live in the greatest Country in the world. How our Country became great is very important to her; she says it should be for all United States Citizens as well.

We have studied every President from George Washington, the Father of our Country, to Dwight D. Eisenhower, the hero of our nation's World War II victory in Europe. My two favorite Presidents are Franklin D. Roosevelt and Dwight D. Eisenhower. Both were leaders who made tough decisions during World War II: Roosevelt, the political and, Eisenhower, the military. Both cared deeply about their fellow citizens and loved the United States Of America. It was interesting to learn how many former military heroes have become successful Presidents of The United States of America. Mrs. Downs says military service teaches leadership, which is mandatory in Presidents. She says the ability to lead our country in difficult times requires strength, tenacity, and perseverance, which some men only learn on the battlefield. I may never be President but I know I want to be a military man some day. I told my Dad my wish, and he said, "Good show, Son. Not everybody is willing to pay that price."

⌘ ⌘ ⌘

Because Dad's occupation as a "Logging Highclimber" was designated a "National Necessity," he was frozen in his job during World War II. Being ineligible for the draft, Dad

General George S. Patton

"I drove to the Rhine River and went across on the pontoon bridge. I stopped in the middle to take a piss and then picked up some dirt on the far side in emulation of William the Conqueror." General George S. Patton, March 1945

General Patton urinates into the Rhine river in Germany

never served in a military uniform while America was fighting the Japanese and the Germans. A number of my Uncles, though, served both in Europe and the Pacific. In fact, my Uncle Sandy was a soldier with General George Patton's Third Army in an Engineers Company that laid the first pontoon bridge across the Rhine River into Germany. Uncle Sandy always took great joy in telling how he watched General Patton take a leak off the pontoon bridge into the Rhine River to show his contempt for Hitler and his vaunted war machine. Uncle

Rock Hill

Sandy said all the American troops nearby cheered Patton's action.

My Uncle Alvin was a Scout for the US Army in Company L, 127th Infantry in the Philippines with Five-Star General Douglas MacArthur. My Mom did tell me that two days a week Dad drove to Vancouver along the Columbia River where, because of his immense knowledge of arranging and rigging steel cables, he helped build the World War II Liberty ships in the Henry J. Kaiser Ship Yards. Mom said the Liberty Ships were vital to shipping supplies and men to the war zones. In his way, she says, "Dad did do his share to help defeat the enemy." Mom says there were many men like Dad who remained at home but still contributed in their own special way to the winning of World War II. She also said millions of women served their Country here at home and overseas as well.

⌘ ⌘ ⌘

Mrs. Downs will not allow anyone to chew gum in class. She says chewing gum is a distraction to learning and fit best for cows and their cud in a field. Bones got caught one time; his penalty was to put the gum on his nose. We all thought it was a rather childish price to pay, but it was funny. Bones says he'd find a way to get even for the humiliation but I suspect he never will. Bones truly likes Mrs. Downs, but he was really embarrassed. One thing, for sure, it usually only happens once to the unfortunate culprit. "Humiliation," Mrs. Downs said, "can be a great Teacher sometimes."

One thing Bones does do quite often is to fart "Silent Sam's". Boy, can that guy launch the worst smells known to man. He always says it is mainly a byproduct of the mustard sandwiches his Mother packs for him. A lot of times we guys pitch in to pay for a hot lunch meal at school so we won't be bombarded by what he calls his "Amazing Lower Colonus." We say the only thing really amazing is what keeps the classroom from catching fire or his classmates from passing out.

Mrs. Downs is either very polite to ignore his gas attacks or just too unsure who the guy is blazing the atmosphere. Surely, though, she hears the groans in the Library when the damage is done. I know she heard Sam Wilcox loudly tell Bones he better go home and change his shorts because he knew Bones had messed his pants. Wilcox, who is always on the verge of being kicked out of school for his loud mouth and classroom shenanigans, has failed to advance a grade a couple of years. Since Washington State Law requires him to either graduate from eighth grade or stay in school until he is at least sixteen years old, Sam is still with us, though he says he would rather be working at a sawmill or serving in the US Army in Korea.

Sometimes Mrs. Downs really glares at Wilcox. But, she lets him get away with a lot because she says it really isn't his fault. He is from a very poor Family. His Father is an alcoholic who occasionally comes to school threatening the School Superintendant while raising an all-around ruckus. Two of his brothers are in Walla Walla State Prison for stealing cars and a sister works in a "House of Pleasure" over in Morton. Bones said, "It is where some men go to drink and have fun with beautiful women." That night at dinner, I asked Dad if he had ever gone to a "House of Pleasure." Mom quickly gave me a sharp look and asked, "Where did you hear that term?" I said, "In Mrs. Downs's class. She was talking about Sam Wilcox's behavior in school that she said was caused by his home environment. Mrs. Downs said Sam's sister worked in a "House of Pleasure" in Morton." Then, Dad said, "Yes, son, but not since I married your Mom, and I have no plans in the future unless your Mother decides to go on a vacation from taking care of her homework." Mom quickly said, "Your Dad has nothing to worry about as long as he keeps his nose headed to the logging camp, his mind on me, and his brains in his pocket." Since both had big smiles on their faces, it sounded to me like a "House Of Pleasure" might be an interesting place to visit some day!

The next time Sam was absent from class while he was illegally jigging for salmon with his Dad, Mrs. Downs told us that Sam was an unfortunate boy who life would chew up and spit out some day. We all should give thanks for the good Families we enjoyed. Believe me, I do! Sam Wilcox sure can make you laugh, though. Once, Sam told Jane he had a pencil in his right pants pocket; Sam claimed he had hurt his right hand while cutting wood at home. He asked her if she would please reach into his pocket to get his pencil. Unbeknown to Jane, Sam had cut the bottom from his pocket. His hammer

JUNIOR HIGH

was hard as a rock, sticking straight up into the pocket. Jane reached for the pencil only to touch his hammer. When she realized what it was, Jane screamed, "You dirty bastard, Wilcox," and got the last laugh by grabbing the shaft and giving it a big pull. I thought old Sam was going to fly through the air. It was really funny! We asked Sam where he got the idea for the pocket stunt. Sam said his brother Craig had learned about the trick while in the county jail. Another jailbird told Craig it worked every time. I guess this jailbird fellow read about how to do it in a book somewhere. Boy, you can read about almost anything in a book! I can't wait until I get old enough to read those kinds of books! Jane White did not tell on Sam, though. Jane did say, "If you pull something like that on me again, you Idiot Wilcox, I will whack your brains in your shorts with a baseball bat." And she will, too!

Another time, Wilcox went above and beyond the call of duty to irritate Mr. Dabney Sweet, who is the most disliked Teacher we've had. He teaches English with joy and hates sports with the same amount of passion. Sam says, "Mr. Sweet walks like he has a bumble bee stuck up his boney ass." Mr. Sweet's great claim to fame is that he graduated from "Havaad" University, a real Mecca of learning in the East somewhere. We guys always resent his "holier than thou attitude." Anyway, Mr. Sweet always makes Wilcox sit alone in a corner away from the rest of us. Mr. Sweet says it's to instill discipline into what definitely would be an otherwise unruly classroom. One day Sam refused to take his seat and threatened to grab Mr. Sweet by his balls and make them ring like Church Bells. When Mr. Sweet complained to the Principal, Wilcox was threatened with another summer at Green Valley Reform School (where Sam said he got beat up every day by a couple of "Hoods.") He grudgingly returned to his corner seat.

Another time Mr. Sweet arrived a minute or two late for class. On his desk was a brown paper box. No one knew what was in it or who put it there. On the box was a card that read: "To My Favorite Teacher." With glee Mr. Sweet said, "Oh, a gift for me! How nice. Let's open it, class, and see what it is." The lid on the box was removed only to reveal a box full of goat turds that stunk to high heaven. Mr. Sweet let out a scream of disbelief, grabbed the box, and headed again to the Principal's office. Mr. Don grilled the class for five minutes about what we saw and when. But it was a waste of time; no proof of Wilcox's guilt ever came to light. We all felt it was just deserts for conceited Mr. Sweet.

Everyone in school including the Principal, however, knew that the Wilcox Family milked goats. In fact, a story about the Wilcox's goats was well known by all the guys and probably some of the girls. Once during P.E., Sam told us he had watched his older brother hammer the old nanny. They were supposed to be only milking the old goat but Sam said his brother Jake got carried away by the fires of youth. He said the nanny couldn't get enough and apparently neither could Jake. We asked Sam how he liked the little beauty when it came his turn, but Sam claimed the nanny didn't care for him so he was unable to judge the quality of goat loving.

The box of goat shit though was almost the undoing of Wilcox. Mr. Sweet put up such a howl over it the School Board finally agreed to exclude Sam from any more of Mr. Sweet's classes. In his defense, Sam said the stink the Teacher raised was far worse than the smell of goat turds.

⌘ ⌘ ⌘

To earn spending money for food at our hangout—Dee's Café, movie tickets at the Z Theater, or athletic equipment in the spring and summer, I mow lawns around town. I don't charge a set price; I just let my customers, our neighbors, tell me what they owe me. That always works pretty well. Most people are more than fair. I use a powered push mower purchased at Damer's Hardware Store. Dad says the activity builds muscle and teaches me the value of a dollar. The toughest job I have is mowing the Rock Hill Cemetery.

Mr. Malley Damer, the owner of Damer's Hardware Store who sits on the Rock Hill Cemetery Board, is my employer. The pay is ten dollars, and it takes all day to mow the entire area. It's not easy to mow around all the gravestones and flower-pots. Sometimes I wonder if some of those people whose names are on the tombstones are sitting on clouds watching me work. I knew and sure miss some of them. When I die if I'm not buried at a US Military Cemetery, I want to be buried at a spot right next to my cousin Jon who was hit and killed by a car driven by a foolish High School boy. I always talk to him when I mow his area. He was known as the "The Singing

Angel" and had long gorgeous hair. Dad thought his hair was way too long, but my Mom loved every lock. We sure miss him. He had such a great sense of humor. Jon was always making my Mom laugh over some silly thing. Like the time he said Mom's sister looked like a cross between Marjorie Main and Marilyn Monroe. Jon said Aunt June had a face that would stop a truck and a pair of boobs that would stop a truck driver.

Another job I have I really like is working at the Getchell Market. Mr. Don got me the job. One of Mr. Don's other jobs in Rock Hill is to cut roasts and steaks for the Getchell Market meat section. Mr. Don says he worked his way through College working part time as a Butcher; now he works part-time at the Getchell Market to earn extra money for his Family. I really like the work at this job because it is inside out of the cold, wet weather. I have many duties at the Market and Dennis and Mary Getchell, the owners, are really fine people. They don't have any children and say they like having a good-hard-working boy to help them out.

The Getchell Market is on the ground floor of the Grange Hall, where dances are held on the second floor on Saturday nights. The Getchells' living quarters are in the rear portion of the building. Between the store in front and the living quarters in the back, is a warehouse section where bulk produce and extra groceries are kept. Off to the side of the store is the meat counter. Nearby is a walk-in freezer where townspeople can rent lockers for storage of fruit, vegetables, and frozen bulk meat, usually wild game or a side of beef raised at home. I am paid twenty-five cents an hour for stocking groceries on the shelf, re-sacking potatoes from hundred-pound burlap bags to five- and ten-pound paper sacks, and sweeping the floors. I also help Mr. Don put cut meat into the refrigerated glass-enclosed meat case. I work an hour each night Monday through Thursday after my paper route is completed and four hours every other Saturday. Mr. Getchell says I am a regular boy wonder and they would have to shut down without my help. I know they are only kidding, but it sounds good.

One time when I was sacking potatoes, a couple of friendly Salesmen came to the Getchell Market. Mr. Getchell introduced them to me; they were really super. Charlie was the Boss, the other a Territory Salesman named Wally. Knowing that I was interested in Airplanes and the Military, Mr. Getchell said Charlie was a US Army Pilot who flew a North American B25 in the South Pacific during World War II. Wally had been a "Dogface" packing an M1 in the US Army during the Korean War. Charlie patted me on the back and said I was just the kind of hardworking guy he always wanted to hire. He asked me if I was interested and winked at Mr. Getchell. He said I would have to relocate and travel a great deal. Then he asked me, "How old are you?" When I said, "fourteen" he replied, "Oh, too bad, the State Of Washington won't let me hire you just yet." He was sure I could handle the job, but Washington State has a law against taking boys out of school too soon. I was supposed to contact him when I graduated from College. He said that he would keep the position

Rock Hill

open until then. I thought the offer was awfully kind though I knew Charlie was only joking.

When Charlie and Wally left, they each shook my hand. As they drove away, I noticed there was a picture of a moon and stars on the side of the car. Mr. Getchell said the Company they represented was an American Institution and their men were the best Salesmen of the Grocery Industry. Mr. Getchell also said the Company's products sold extremely well. He said a store would lose customers if their products were not readily available for Mrs. Housewife.

One incident happened while I was working at Getchell's Market that is unforgettable. A cereal company named for some General named Mills that made a "Breakfast Food For Champions" offered a drawing for a free collegiate model football. I helped Mr. Getchell create the display for the promotion. We stacked boxes of the breakfast cereal around a card table that had a box sitting on it. The box had a slit where box tops from the cereal boxes were deposited. Each contestant wrote his or her name on the tops. The more tops in the box, the greater chance a participant had to win.

Boy, I wanted to win that football. Since I was at the store every day, I looked through the slot to see all my tops. I just knew I was going to win. In fact, I bragged to any one who would listen. I thought I had the football won hands down. When I told Mr. Getchell how confident I was about winning, he said to me, "Do not to be so sure, for the road of life sometimes takes an unusual turn." I said, "Nope, I know it is in the bag. Or in the box, you might say." Well, lo and behold, when the Saturday rolled around to open the box and count the tops, guess what happened? Yep, you guessed it: I lost.

Larry Boyd, a Preacher's kid, won it with forty tops to my twenty-three. I always thought he had "Divine Help", but it didn't matter. I was empty handed. Mr. Getchell told me it was a pure case of my counting my chickens before they hatched. "However," Mr. Getchell also said, **"you probably won the greatest prize: A Lesson In Humility. Never count on something until you actually have it in your possession. Don't brag about something unless it has come to pass. Only a fool needlessly embarrasses himself. Smart people earn recognition through quiet adherence to duty, honor, and hard work. Sometimes, however, foolish people have to learn life's lessons through loss, as well as achievement."**

Of all my jobs in Rock Hill that I have had over the years, the one I am most proud of is being a *Seattle Times* newspaper boy. For two years now, I have delivered the *Seattle Times* to seventy-five daily and eighty Sunday customers in and around Rock Hill. When I was selected for the job, Dad said, "It is a real feather in your cap. It is also a serious responsibility that you have accepted. It is important that you do your best to make the Blethen Family satisfied." I asked, "Who are the Blethens?"

"The Blethens," Dad said, "are one of the finest newspaper Families in the United States. They are historic, on a par with the Sulzberger Family, who are the publishers of the *New York Times*; the Hearst Family, who own papers from New York to San Francisco; the Chandler Family, who own the *Los*

Angeles Times; the Newhouse Family who own the *Portland Oregonian*, my favorite newspaper; and even Horace Greely who wrote 'Go West, Young Man' and founded and edited the *New York Tribune*. The patriarch, Colonel Blethen, moved here from the State of Maine, bought the paper in 1896, and helped develop Seattle by publishing the *Seattle Times*. Remember, Jim, the *Seattle Times* Company only hires hard workers and will be expecting a lot from you. Believe me, it will be a challenge." And it is!

I asked Mom how Dad knows so much about the newspaper industry. Mom said, "Dad is a 'voracious' reader and read a book about newspaper history in our Country." I asked Mom what "voracious" meant. She said, "It means Dad has a huge appetite for, among other things, reading." Dad was listening to us, and he smiled at Mom and said, "Especially other things!" Boy, I really don't know sometimes about their conversations; it seems like they talk to one another without really saying everything!

Monday through Saturday, I ride my bicycle with a *Seattle Times* canvas newspaper sack attached to the handle bars to carry the papers. It's hard work and it takes me about an hour and a half to complete my route. On Sunday, because the papers are heavier, my Mom drives me around my route in her car to make the deliveries.

My Dad said, "You are in business for yourself. Not only do you have to deliver papers but you must also collect the money from your customers for the papers. It is up to you alone to see that the route is profitable. Remember, a business

Dad was a very smart man who learned by doing and reading. He always said, "Never ask a man to do what you would not do." Equaling his accomplishments and ability was never a possibility for Jim

that loses money has to shut down. The *Seattle Times* is depending on you to be a good steward of their Sales Territory. You will succeed or fail based on your management skills and dedication to the job."

Mrs. Downs , my History Teacher, said in class that my job as a Newspaper Delivery Boy is one of the most important in Rock Hill. She said it is very crucial for town citizens to be well informed about current events. America's newspapers are the primary communication medium by which local people can stay well informed about national, state, and local news. She said in a Republic such as the United States it is imperative that citizens know what the government is doing in their lives. In a free society like America, it is vital that people have access to the truth, as can be determined by a Professional Newspaper Writer who investigates, writes objectively, and then prints the facts in his or her newspaper stories.

We actually have three other daily papers that are distributed in Rock Hill: (1) the *Portland Oregonian*, (2) the *Tacoma News Tribune*, and (3) the *Centralia Daily Chronicle* for Lewis County news. In addition, two weekly papers are mailed: the *Chehalis Advocate*, which emphasizes farm news, and the *Morton Journal*, which features local news and sports of East Lewis County. Dad says, "Rock Hill is very fortunate to be so well covered by the newspaper industry. If anyone is in the dark about issues facing our Citizens, it is only because that person is either too lazy to read or unfortunately unable. I am proud of the job you do to help keep the people of Rock Hill up to date with what is currently happening in our world."

In a way, our Family on my Dad's side has a background in the newspaper industry. Aunt Agnes (my Dad's sister), who my Dad says is a frustrated housewife turned business woman, began in the newspaper business working as a Writer and an Advertising Salesperson for the *Kelsoian*, a weekly paper in Kelso. Soon, she took a Sales Management position traveling the West Coast for the Liner Circulation Company, running newspaper circulation sales contests. The Summer after my sixth grade, Aunt Agnes came to the *Chehalis Advocate* to put on a sales contest. The first person she contacted was

Dad, asking to let me enter the contest by selling subscriptions in Eastern Lewis County. Dad said, "Yes." Mom said, "No." Aunt Agnes talked to my Mom and, with a woman's plea to another woman, persuaded Mom to change her mind. For a month Mom drove me around Eastern Lewis County every day during the sales campaign.

Apparently, the *Chehalis Advocate* was having a difficult time remaining in business because its circulation had fallen to a level that caused a serious reduction in advertising revenue. A newspaper needs both advertising and subscription revenue to operate at a profit and remain in business. Aunt Agnes said, "Greater circulation numbers drive increased advertising rates and sales, creating greater revenue." The Liner Circulation sales contest, it was hoped, would lead to a more profitable *Chehalis Advocate* Newspaper Company.

My Aunt Agnes is a very intelligent, articulate woman who is devoted to the newspaper business. She said, "Every citizen in town should subscribe to the local paper to help it remain in business. American newspapers are the primary source of honest information for Citizens about what the government is doing for, with, and sometimes, to us. To preserve our way of life and help keep his local Gazette in business, a person should buy the local paper even if he only uses it to line the bottom of a bird cage." Dad said he is proud of his sister and told me to listen carefully to what she says about business in general and advertising in particular.

When the sales contest was over, with Mom's help in driving me around, I had sold over 100 hundred new subscriptions.

Rock Hill

I won a Wilcox wire recorder and a one-hundred-dollar US Savings Bond! The wire recorder was fun to use to either practice oral class reports or to make believe I am a radio sports show interviewer. During the sales campaign, I met many wonderful people throughout the Eastern Lewis County. I was pleased that Aunt Agnes was satisfied with my results. She told Dad, "Jim will make a good living using his smile and sales ability. When Jim is older, he will have a fine future if he gets a sound education and remains committed to always trying to do his best."

Before she left Rock Hill, Aunt Agnes told Dad that she was concerned about the future of newspapers in America. With television developing and broadcast radio in its zenith, newspaper advertising was under attack. She said newspapers supported by advertising are absolutely necessary for a free United States. A free press is a constitutional right that is one of the pillars of our way of life. The newspaper industry will always be the primary source of unbiased information by which American citizens can judge the honesty, effectiveness, and common sense of the United States Government. Dad said he was very proud of his sister's accomplishments. Mom said, "Aunt Agnes represents many women who would like to excel in a position outside the home. One day perhaps society will realize that raising children is not the only career some women desire. I know many women who feel their life is almost a total waste because housekeeping is such an incomplete and inadequate use of their talent and abilities."

⌘ ⌘ ⌘

My Mom told me her family knew loss and hard times when she was a young girl. Our extended family had come to the State of Washington from the Ozarks of Missouri and Arkansas. A half brother had first left home to find work for everyone. Initially, Uncle Earl worked in the oil fields of Oklahoma and Texas; then, he hopped on a freight train in Colorado headed for the Pacific Northwest. In a little spot on the road called Stella, West of Longview along the Ocean Beach Highway, Uncle Earl found work for most of the family. Grandpa was a Blacksmith and got a job as an Auto Mechanic. My Mom and Grandma cleaned a small hotel and clerked in a little country store. On Saturday nights, they also worked in a dance hall built on a dock sitting on piling in the Columbia River. The dance hall was on the second floor of the building, and Grandpa's garage was on the ground floor.

For a time, my Uncles all played in the country music dance band. Mom says she was raised on country music. Her Father and Brothers all played guitars and fiddles. At Grandpa and Grandma's home anytime there was a family get-together there was always music in the living room after dinner. My Grandpa and my Uncles knew all the old standards like Gene Autry's *"You Are My Sunshine,"* Jimmie Rodgers's *"Peach-Pickin' Time Down in Georgia,"* Bob Wills's *"San Antonio Rose,"* and Roy Acuff's *"Wabash Cannon Ball."* Those who wanted to dance did. My Dad, who insisted that he was allergic to music and dancing, always sat in a corner reading a book.

On Saturday nights, they always took time to listen to the Grand Ole Opry from Nashville, Tennessee, on the radio. The program featured great country music and tied Mom's family to their roots. Lord have mercy, though, if a grandchild raised a fuss while the show was on the air. Grandpa's blue eyes could ice over lightning fast if the ruckus continued for more than ten seconds. Grandpa could also threaten to get his leather strap to quiet any "little idiot" quicker than anyone I know.

Although Grandpa gave Sam Wilcox's Dad a good run for his money for threatening to use the belt, Sam's Dad took the grand prize when it came to actually applying the punishment. Mom used to always say that Grandpa, for all his bluster sometimes, was really a kind--hearted person who loved his grandchildren very much. I said, "Yes, but I sure heard him get upset one time when he was talking with Grandma one night in bed." Mom, who loved her Mother very much and thought Grandpa didn't show Grandma enough respect sometimes, raised her voice and sharply asked, "What about?" I told her, "Well, Grandpa was angry about Cousin Sid when Sid visited in the summertime. Grandpa said, "Sid was fifteen years old and still messing the sheets at night, for heaven's sake. Why can't the little feller get out of bed and walk five feet to the porch and wiz into the grass? He's just too lazy to get out of bed!" Mom then asked, "What did Grandma say?" I said, "Grandma just told Grandpa to mind his own business. He didn't have to clean it up and that Sid would eventually grow out of it." I also said, "There is one thing for sure, none of Sid's cousins ever want to sleep in the same bed with him!"

My Mother loved to dance and listen to country music. My Father truly didn't care for either. Dad said, "My idea of a great Saturday night is to rest by the living-room fire, read a good book, and mind my own business." Dad absolutely did not care for drinking or loud people. He always said dance halls and his in-laws' living room featured both. Mom loved Dad very much and said, "My dancing slippers were put up on the shelf when I married your Dad." I was to be her Fred Astaire in waiting. She said, "You can dance for both of us."

The Saturday-night Grange Hall Dance in Rock Hill had been a curiosity for me ever since I'd spent time with my old gang finding empty beer bottles in the parking area on Sunday mornings. Music is provided by a local country western band. Hoot Greuter and his Tune Squeezers sound like a cross between Hank Thompson and Webb Pierce. Molly Givins, the girl singer, can sing and cry just like Patsy Cline.

Few Junior High boys go to Saturday-night dances. About the only time our Family attends is the night of the Fireman's Ball. Dad says it is a civic duty to support the Rock Hill Volunteer Fire Department. Every ticket sold is another dollar in the firehouse treasury. Of course about half of the Junior High girls attend regularly, usually as dates of older High School boys. Jane White is always there and is known as a good bet to leave the dance hall during intermission when the band takes a half-hour break. Her reputation for necking and petting is roundly discussed by the boys.

Bones said that one time at a dance, he walked by a car Jane was in. The windows were down, she was in the back seat, her feet were pointed toward the roof, and she was saying, "Damn it, Jack, keep that little thing in, will you?" Apparently, Jack had had one too many bottles of Olympia Beer. He laughingly told Jane to "grab Big Tommy and give him a hand." Jane told the fellow, "Go to hell!" She opened the door, got out, pulled up her panties, and slammed the door. As Jane walked by Bones, Jane said, "What are you doing, Bones, sneaking a peak for a thrill?" Then, she laughed and headed back to the dance.

I learned to dance at my Classmate Carol Deed's home. By Junior High, the Deed Family had moved into Rock Hill from a farm outside of town. In the fifth grade when I used to walk back home from the Rock Hill Airport, sometimes I would stop at the Deed farm to visit with Carol, her older Sister Tara and Mrs. Deed. I did not do it very often, though, because Mom was really strict about my being home on time. Also, the Deed girls could be really mischievous at times; I always had to be on guard. Tara and Carol loved to wrestle, and both of them together could get me down and either refuse to let me up or take my jacket and refuse to give it back because they did not want me to leave yet. One time, Mrs. Deed had to come to my rescue by threatening to whip both girls with a Willow Switch that Carol said, "hurt like mad." Another time, I was so upset with myself because I was not strong enough to get the girls off me, and I reached for Carol's pony-tail and gave it a really hard pull. Darn if she didn't sock me hard right on my jaw, just like a boy. I swear I saw stars. It really hurt, but I would never ever let Carol or Tara or anyone in The Gang know that I was knocked out by a girl, for heaven's sake!

Mina Deed is a short lady with a bouncy personality. She loves her husband, Jerry, two daughters, Tara and Carol, and son, Berl. Classmate Carol Deed is really a good friend, I like her a lot. Anything the kids want to do that is fun and wholesome is all right with Jerry. He worships Mina, and is all for anything Mina wants. Since Mina lives to dance, she thought her daughters should learn how as well. Lessons started in the seventh grade. At first we boys were shy and unsure if dancing was something worth trying. Of course the girls were all in favor. The Deeds had an RCA Victor console phonograph with two speakers, and a stack of 78, 33 1/3, and 45 RPM records. Bing Crosby, Perry Como, Glen Miller, Benny Goodman, Doris Day, Roy Acuff, and Kitty Wells were some of the Artists. Tara Deed's birthday party one Saturday afternoon was the occasion of the first lesson. Mina Deed paired the group (six boys and six girls), put Nat King Cole's record of *"Too Young"* on the phonograph, and then, said, "Take two steps forward, one step backward. Just slide across the floor like this." Then, Jerry and Mina showed us how.

Mina said, "take the girl's hand like so and put the other hand around her back." Boy, this looked pretty good if a guy could just learn the steps. After a few dances it got a little easier. Sure there was a lot of stepping on toes, banging into knees, and bumping into each other, but the fun was real.

The ultimate goal was to get so good at slow dancing that the move to jitterbugging would be automatic. Jerry and Mina could really jitterbug. In fact, Tara Deed, the older sister, told us that her Parents had won a trophy and a free trip to Reno at a regional dance contest when they were young. We had no doubt because the Deeds could really "shake a leg," as Carol said. Jerry Deed had been a Marine during World War II, having fought at Guadalcanal where he had been shot in the right leg just above the knee. "Two inches higher and that damn Jap would have ended my chances of having this beautiful Family," he always joked. Jerry had obviously recovered well because the way Mina and Jerry dance together is fantastic. They are very nice people and very good dance teachers. Jerry encouraged the guys and Mina the girls.

Throughout the seventh grade we developed our dancing skills at every opportunity: birthdays, a Halloween party, occasionally at school during a rare co-ed   P.E. class, and, even rarer, Junior High sock dances. By eighth grade, most boys and girls are pretty good dancers. I can two-step, waltz, polka, schottische, and jitterbug fairly well. All the girls say I have good rhythm. Even my Mom says I am pretty handy on the dance floor. She is always trying to get me to dance with her because Dad refuses. Mom said it would take three beers and a fifth of whiskey just to get him off his butt to dance. And truth be told, Dad NEVER drinks.

In the eighth grade, the most important dances are off limits to us, especially the girls: the Rock Hill High School Sock Dances. The boys are considered too young and the girls too much competition! Jane White and Flo Brown are always trying to sneak in. As soon as a Junior or Senior girl spots them on the dance floor, they are told to leave. Once, Jane got in trouble for telling Mrs. Wilma Baxter, the Home Economics Teacher and sock dance chaperone, to kiss her where the sun doesn't shine. Unfortunately, that response only hastened her exit and initiated a bawling out for "talking trash" by Mr. Don at school on Monday morning.

Everyone in the class really likes Flo Brown. She is a really good-looking girl who is very smart and has a terrific sense of humor. Flo is a Negro girl whose Father moved to Rock Hill to work at the dam being constructed on the Cowlitz River. Flo and Jane act like sisters. Sometimes they even dress alike. The two girls could not be more different in looks: Jane is a gorgeous blue--eyed blonde, while Flo is a dark-haired, dark--skinned beauty. The High School fellows are always trying to get Flo and Jane to go out with them. Flo says she plans to be a Baby Doctor someday, and Jane says she hopes someday to keep a Baby Doctor busy. Who knows, maybe they will help each other be successful in life.

I had lunch one time at the Brown Family home after mowing their lawn. Boy, can Mrs. Brown cook! She made the best hamburger I ever tasted. We had corn on the cob, too. Mrs. Brown gave me a dollar tip because she said I had mowed her lawn like a real Professional Gardener. I was really pleased. In the living room of the Brown's mobile home there was a picture prominently displayed of a Black American Aviator standing by a North American P-51 with a Red Tail. I asked

Mrs. Brown who the Pilot was. She said it was her brother Raymond, Flo's Uncle, who flew in the 332nd Fighter Group of the 15th Air Force during World War II in one of the Famous Black Fighter Squadrons: The Tuskegee Airmen. Those Black Aviators lost very few USAF Bombers to German Fighters on bombing runs over France and Germany. American Bomber Crews called the Black Fighter Squadrons the "Red Tail Angels."

I was really impressed, and I asked Mrs. Brown if Uncle Raymond ever visited. She said, "Yes", and I told her I would love to meet him someday because he was a true War Hero and had to be an outstanding Combat Pilot. Mrs. Brown said that she would try to get us together. But, unfortunately, we never met. Flo's Father, Mr. Brown, who was a Civil Engineer working for the construction company that was building the Rock Hill Dam, was transferred to a job in another state before Uncle Raymond could visit.

Having Flo Brown in our History Class, though, was a true education in itself. One summer vacation she lived in Mississippi with her Grandmother. She told the class about a way of life that was completely different from the one in Rock Hill. Flo described things that made absolutely no sense to us. She told about separate restrooms with signs above each door that read: "FOR WHITES ONLY and FOR COLORED ONLY." Whole schools, too, were just for one race or the other. Flo said race separation or segregation, as it was called in the South, was the accepted law of the land throughout the Southern United States Of America.

JUNIOR HIGH

A Red Tail Angel on Patrol and The Tuskegee Airman Logo

139

Rock Hill

All of the class listened in disbelief at Flo's stories of crimes and atrocities that were committed against Black American Citizens that local law enforcement refused to investigate, arrest, or prosecute. The class asked, "What about the Constitution that says all Citizens are created equal? The Bill Of Rights, too, don't they apply to all United States Citizens in the South?" Flo said, "No, those documents may exist, but it doesn't mean Southern Officials abide by them." Flo told Jane that if a Black man even looked at, or actually touched Jane's body in a lustful way, if he were caught, the Black man might be badly beaten, or even lynched by White men wearing white robes. Hung from a tree like a cattle rustler in the Old West, would you believe! Truly, it was hard to understand how such mistreatment could happen in this day and age to fellow American Citizens.

The class asked Mrs. Downs why the U.S. Government didn't do something to force the Southern States to obey the Constitution. Mrs. Downs said, "Segregation indeed is a national tragedy. Almost a hundred years ago even a Civil War, where over six hundred thousand Americans died on the battlefield, failed to solve the shameful problem. Mrs. Downs said, "It is up to you younger Citizens of United States to overcome hate, greed, and outright meanness to change the hearts of some White people to make the lives of Black American Citizens better." Mrs. Downs added, "Truth be told, the mistreatment of Racial Minorities is not just a problem in the South. Discrimination exists throughout the United States; please be aware of this terrible fact."

The whole class thought Flo Brown moved away all too soon. We really valued Flo's brains, beauty, and genuine friendship. The class was really sad when her Dad received a transfer to a new dam being built somewhere in Idaho. Jane cried for over a week when she learned Flo was moving. So did a number of the fellows in our class and the High School as well, I am sure.

I like music of all types: country western, popular, blues, and jazz. As long as the music has a good beat, I can always shake a leg pretty good. Music by Frank Sinatra is always very popular; we can't wait to hear his latest record. Anything by Frankie Lane, Perry Como, Hank Williams, The Four Aces, Harry James, or Patti Page can cause a boy to look for a partner. I have Jerry and Mina Deed to thank for setting my feet to moving in time with the music on the dance floor.

One thing I really like about dancing is getting to hold a girl close. I like to smell their aroma. Some girls use perfume that really smells great. Jane says, "Evening in Paris" is very popular. Some girls put it on their necks and their arms. The guys wondered how many put it on their legs. Jane proudly said, "I do." She says it's a grown-up way of doing the right thing. She said she never wants any of her smells to offend anyone. In band once, Bones, Jane, and I were talking between songs about dancing when the subject of perspiration arose. Bones offered to help Jane put perfume on some time. Jane told him to, "just dream on, midget." I said that was funny because Bones is really tall for his age. Jane said she meant something else. Bones said she'd be surprised. Jane got a sly smile on her face, and we all had a laugh.

Being close to a girl while dancing can sometimes cause problems, though. I try not to think about romantic things too much. One time when I was dancing with Penny Waddles, my hammer began to rise, and it began to stick right straight out. Talk about embarrassing! Penny knew what was going on too; she kept pushing herself against me. Gee, my face was getting warm and probably red as well. I said, "Boy, it's getting hot in here, Penny," as I pulled myself away. The only problem was my hammer stuck right straight out. It was really embarrassing! Finally in one fell swoop I did a solo turn on my heels right in time with the music and with one hand I hit my hammer straight up and completed the turn to take Penny in my arms again. Pretty slick move! Penny moved close to me, but she knew immediately the object of her interest had relocated. I must say she had a disappointed look on her face. I just smiled at the thought of my fancy footwork!

⌘ ⌘ ⌘

Dee's Café is the social hangout in Rock Hill for almost everyone in school. Dee's menu features hamburgers, French fries, pie, soft ice cream, milk shakes of all flavors, and fountain drinks from the tap. The restaurant is in the front of Dee's remodeled home. Dee Fender and her husband, Goney, live in the back. She is about five feet tall and weighs over two hundred pounds, a testament to her good cooking and lack of exercise.

There are five or six tables in the main part of the café, a pinball machine, and a jukebox that plays 45 RPM records for five cents each or six for a quarter. Pictures of Coca-Cola products in pleasing scenes hang on the walls. There is also a counter with stools where customers can sit to eat. Candy bars and chewing gum are kept on shelves behind the counter. Cream and berry pies are kept in a vertical showcase that sits on the edge of the counter by the cash register. A soft ice cream machine sits on the floor between the dining area and the kitchen. Off to the side behind a wall, there is a cozy dining room where the Lions Club meets monthly. High School students are allowed to go to Dee's Café during the school day at lunch-time. Junior High students are not. We always show up after school or on weekends when hunger or boredom calls. There is always either a new pinball game to play, a new record to hear, or some friend to meet.

Betty West and Faye Wise are the waitresses. Both are older women who have been divorced and relish teasing the boys about "stepping out" with them or helping the girls with their "man" problems. Both wear white uniforms and have pretty good figures for older women. They smell of sexy perfume and wear makeup to look like movie stars. By the way, Betty West is one beautiful woman who is a good friend of my Mom. Betty was the wife of Doc West, one of Rock Hill's Aviators and a very good friend of my Dad. Also, Betty's sister, Marilyn, is married to Gus Thompson, a Rock Hill

Rock Hill

genuine military hero. During World War II, Gus was a tail gunner on a B-17 that was shot down over Germany. Gus was imprisoned in a German POW camp for two years. After his release, Gus's picture and story were featured in *Life* magazine. The whole town was happy over the wonderful news of his release. He now works as the High School Janitor. Everyone in Rock Hill loves both Gus and Marilyn.

All of us know Dee Fender is a Saint who never turns a deaf ear to a student in need. If you are broken in spirit and hungry, Dee will always spot you a burger, fries, a drink, and encouragement. The High School students have credit at Dee's Café but not those in Junior High. Dee says we are not old enough to value the responsibility that credit creates. Neither does she wish to antagonize Parents who wouldn't approve of the arrangement. Dee Fender is never one to let a boy or girl go hungry, though. More than one student from a poor Family has been given a meal to tide them over. My buddy, Terry Bones, is always getting a milk shake on the cuff. As a last resort to collect payment, Dee's husband Goney makes sure Bones works off his bill by hoeing and pulling weeds in the café flower garden.

Goney Fender is a sight to see. Six feet tall, white haired, with wire-rimmed glasses, he is an imposing figure. In charge of road maintenance for Rock Hill, he is also a part-time City Policeman assisting Chief Earl Horton. The High School boys call the two officers "Fearless Fender" and "J. Edgar Horton." Always on the lookout for teenage mischief, Goney has a terrible time tolerating the antics of some High School students.

For sure, Goney can't stand to have a guy raise the volume on the jukebox without his permission. He also keeps a sharp eye on the pinball machine to make sure a player doesn't use a slug or put the machine on his toes to control the flow of the ball by leveling the playing area. If a machine hits a certain figure, free games are earned. Goney says, "You cheat the machine, you cheat the café; to cheat the café is ultimately to cheat the player of his just rewards. In other words, you do not win any free games. You must remember that growing up is the time all young people should learn honesty is the only policy. Life will not tolerate a thief." Some of the High School boys act like they are playing a sad tale of woe on a harp when Goney begins to preach. We all know he is right; we just don't like his Sermon or condescending manner of delivery.

Believe me, the boss of Dee's Café is Dee Fender. Although she is a truly kind person, I have seen her put the verbal snap on a few kids if she thinks pranks are being pulled. Pouring unwanted ketchup on someone else's food, mixing the contents of the salt and pepper shakers, or unscrewing the lids on the shakers so the entire contents dump on the unsuspecting diner's food are all stunts guaranteed to cause Dee to unload on someone. Pull one too many tricks and a loss of credit or even banishment for a period of time will result. One thing for sure, absolutely no foul language is ever tolerated. If Goney Fender hears a dirty word among the hamburgers, French fries, or onion rings, pity the poor fool he has overheard—boy or girl. Goney will point toward the door, and

Rock Hill

the culprit better be quick about leaving. Sometimes, though, Goney can be too strict in his interpretation of café rules of proper conduct and Dee will get upset. More than once Dee has told Goney to "get back to the Family Room and leave my customers alone. The café is mine, and I am the boss, and you better be darn quick about minding your own business!" Of course when it happens, every student in the café has a big smile on his face. There is nothing better than to see and hear the watchdog being reprimanded!

My favorite meal at Dee's is a hot roast beef sandwich: a thick piece of roast beef between two pieces of white bread with melt-in-your-mouth mashed potatoes covered with rich brown gravy, a vegetable (corn, peas, or green beans), and a salad with French dressing. I always have a glass of cold milk, too. The price is $1.55 (twenty-five cents extra if you add pie and soft ice cream). The bill can wipe out your budget for the week, but the taste of the food is worth it. Most of the time I just have a hamburger, French fries made from fresh potatoes with the skins still on, and a chocolate milk shake. When I have the extra money, I always have a piece of blueberry pie smothered in soft vanilla ice cream. That is a meal fit for a King. I play the pinball machine once in a while, too, but Mom says it is a form of gambling that could lead to addiction and she prefers I don't. "There will be plenty of time for you to roll dice later in life; I don't need you to start gambling before you even graduate from Junior High for Heaven's sake," she said.

Dee's Café is our home away from home, the center of social activity outside of school, and source of food for hungry growing boys and girls facing starvation. Life would be difficult without Dee Fender's love and care for young people. Sometimes our Moms and Dads are too close to the problems to consider more than one solution. "My way or the highway" is not something a boy or girl wants to hear, even if the statement is mostly in jest. When problems develop at home or school, Betty, Faye and Dee are always ready to listen, reassure, and lend a helping hand. Yes, Dee's Café makes growing up a lot easier and certainly more fun.

⌘ ⌘ ⌘

The Z Theater in Rock Hill is where everyone goes for motion picture entertainment. "It's our little part of Hollywood," as Mom says. The name comes from the first letter of the name of the people who own the business, the Zeddas. They are from Lebanon in the Middle East. Mr. Horace Zedda came to America in the early 1900's. He did pretty well, too! The Zeddas also own one of the Rock Hill's three grocery stores, a food cannery, and a hotel.

Harry Zedda is one of my best friends. He was a very important member of The Gang I was in when we were younger. The Zeddas are of the Catholic Faith. Many nights I have heard Harry and his older brother Ike say their prayers called Beads with their Mother. It always seems like they say the same thing over and over again. It must work because the Zedda family sure doesn't want for anything.

Marie Zedda is a great cook. Their home always has such rich and strange smells coming from the kitchen. Beautiful thick and soft rugs cover the floors. On the living room walls hang portraits of Aunts and Uncles overseas in the Old Country. Harry says, "It's how my Dad and Mom keep in touch mentally with our relatives while living far away."

Mr. Zedda is quite a bit older than his wife. After making his fortune in America, he returned to the Old Country to find a bride. Mrs. Zedda is considered an exotic beauty, and the townspeople love her. She is always very nice to me. She makes old Harry toe the mark, though. On more than one occasion I have seen Mrs. Zedda "slap some sense" into poor Harry. In fact, Harry starts ducking when his Mother starts a conversation with, "I'm going to slap some sense into you, Harry."

Mrs. Zedda sells the tickets at the Z Theater. One admission is twenty cents. Three different movies play weekly. The same picture plays on Tuesday and Wednesday nights, usually a "B" rated movie, as Harry calls it. More often than not it is a Gene Autry, Hopalong Cassidy, or Roy Rogers and Dale Evans picture that attracts the Family audience. Sometimes there is also the next chapter of my favorite "*Tailspin Tommy*" serial that runs. We cannot wait to see how *"Tailspin"* gets out of his latest predicament. A more popular movie plays Friday and Saturday nights. Sunday nights are reserved for what Harry calls: "A Blockbuster."

"Bend of the River" with Jimmy Stewart was "A Blockbuster," The Z Theater was sold out because the motion picture had been filmed near Portland around spectacular Mt. Hood. Since many people in town read the *Portland Oregonian*, the filming of the movie could be followed through stories in the paper. Fans were not disappointed either. *"Bend of the River"* was a thrilling story about a wagon train on its way to the Willamette Valley in Oregon. The movie scenery was filmed in Technicolor and was gorgeous. Jimmy Stewart was excellent in his portrayal of the trail boss. I especially like Jimmy Stewart because he was a heroic USAF B-24 pilot during World War II. A fan would never guess such a fact by the way Mr. Stewart acts. He is not a braggart, that's for sure.

Another great movie that packed the Z Theater and actually had patrons sitting in the aisles was *"Scudda Hoo! Scudda Hey!,"* a mountain family story set in the hills of Kentucky. The plot revolved around farming with mules and starred June Haver, Lon McCallister, and Walter Brennan. Because of the story, locale and Actors, there was great interest in this show. Many residents who live around Rock Hill are descendents of some who migrated west from the Southern United States after the Civil War to make a better living in the Pacific Northwest. *"Scudda Hoo! Scudda Hey!"* presented an opportunity for those folks to return to thoughts of loved ones and scenes of bygone days. *"On the Trail of the Lonesome Pine"* with Henry Fonda, Sylvia Sidney, and Fred MacMurray was another great movie about Southerners. It caused home-sickness for many in Rock Hill for the great State of

Rock Hill

Kentucky and was sold out, too. As a mater of fact, Rock Hill even has several members of the famous Hatfield Family of the well known Eastern Kentucky Hatfield - McCoy feud. Slim Hatfield, a Cat Skinner, has worked for many years off and on for my Dad and Uncle Sandy in the woods.

By far, the two most popular movies that have ever played at the Z Theater were, **FIRST**, *"Since You Went Away"* with Claudette Colbert, Jennifer Jones, Shirley Temple, Robert Walker, and Joseph Cotten, which was the story of the home front during World War II. Almost everyone in Rock Hill had a loved one or friend in the War, and everyone did all they could to help in the war effort here at home. Mom and Dad said the whole town cried when news was received of the loss of a loved one overseas.

And **SECOND** *"Gone with The Wind,"* starring Clark Gable, Vivian Leigh, Thomas Mitchell, Leslie Howard, and Olivia de Havilland. The famous Black actress Hattie McDaniel was featured in both films. "Gone with the Wind" was about one of the most difficult times in American history: the Civil War. Or as my Classmate Flo Brown says, "The War Between the States, if you are a Southerner." Since many of Rock Hill's citizens had Grandfathers and Great Uncles who fought for both the North and South, there was great interest in this spectacular motion picture.

Both movies were produced by Mr. David O. Selznick, a man of the Jewish Faith who all of Rock Hill said had to be a very patriotic Hollywood Executive who had a great love for his Country, The United States Of America. Mom was really affected by these movies. She said during World War II she prayed many times that God would bring home her brothers safely. Mom also said our Family was a typical American Family: Her Ancestors fought for General Robert E. Lee and the Stars and Bars of the Confederacy. Dad's Family on his Mother's side were all Soldiers in the Union Army fighting for the Red, White, and Blue and General Ulysses S. Grant.

Harry and his brother Ike each work nightly at the theater. Ike runs the projector and Harry operates the refreshment stand. You can buy popcorn, candy, or soda pop. Harry claims the popcorn is made fresh daily with all unsold popcorn discarded nightly. Rock Hill High School boys always tease Harry and Ike about the Zedda family's reputation for not wasting a penny. They accuse Harry and Ike of keeping the unsold popcorn overnight and using the pet cat to keep it warm between showings. (Old Tom stays in the theater to eliminate the mice population.) The fellows say that when the movie is over and the Z Theater is empty, Old Tom crawls into the popcorn machine to sleep on the softest, warmest bed in town. One patron, allegedly, said that his throat was blanketed with cat hair from just one bag of popcorn; and it took a vacuum cleaner to remove all the hair and rescue the man from suffocation. Everyone always laughs at that story, except of course, Harry and Ike. Actually, Dad and Mom say the Zeddas are extra honest in their dealings with others and operate super clean businesses.

Prior to the main feature, The Z Theater shows (1) Previews of coming attractions, (2) Movie Tone News which

Rock Hill

shows what is going on in the world, (3) A Mickey Mouse or Bugs Bunny Cartoon, and (4) At certain times a "Short": This "Short" encourages a donation to the March of Dimes or some other Charity.

Once on a Movie Tone News clip we saw pictures and heard a story about the US Navy Destroyer "HOEL" in the South Pacific during The Battle of Leyte Gulf in World War II. Uncle Earl's son Harold served aboard the "HOEL," as a Deck Officer. Rock Hill Citizens and Cousin Harold's loved ones were really proud and prayed that he would return from combat unharmed.

When Charity nights occur, the Z Theater stops the movie, the lights are turned on, and containers are passed to collect donations. Occasionally, I am selected to help pass a container from row to row. I always consider this act an honor and feel I am helping heal sick boys and girls across America. During World War II, U.S. Savings Bonds and Stamps were sold during intermission. The Zeddas say they were very proud to have had their theater play an important economic role in the defense of America, which they love dearly. The Zedda Family knows the United States of America has been very good to them. Dad and Mom say the Zedda Family has been very good for this Country and the town of Rock Hill, as well.

I especially like the news segments about sports and aviation. Actually, Bugs Bunny and Elmer Fudd are my favorite cartoon characters. We go to the movies almost three times a week because it is our only form of entertainment, especially during the wintertime when darkness comes early. The only time we don't go is when there is a game at the Rock Hill High School.

Television is just starting to be received in Rock Hill. The Zedda Family is one of the first Families in town who own a set. Three stations come in from Seattle, but reception is poor. Something called ghosts are always appearing on the screen. The Zeddas think because there are few sets in the area, television isn't much competition for the Z Theater now. However, Mr. Zedda says, "One should always keep a sharp eye on the future. In America, change can happen overnight!"

In Seattle, Horace Zedda has investments in an insurance company, the food industry, and banking. Mr. Zedda is very frugal and rules the Family with an iron hand covered with a velvet glove. In the Zedda Family, his word is not only a command, it is the law. Mrs. Zedda obeys him without question. Their relationship is sure different from my Parents' marriage. Boy, on more than one occasion I have heard my Mother tell my Father to go soak his head when she objects to something he says. My Mother is a handful for my Dad. They get along pretty well, but Mother says it is because she doesn't hesitate to straighten my Father out on a few things. Dad says it is because he always lets Mom think she is the boss. At that remark, my Mom just laughs. I always wonder what my Parents' marriage would be like if Dad had some of Mr. Zedda's temperament in him, and Mom was more like Mrs. Zedda.

The Zedda Family is a true American success story. It is said Mr. Zedda arrived in New York City with little money in his pocket but a great deal of desire and determination

Rock Hill

to succeed. My Dad said, **"Mr. Zedda's story is a far cry from some today who expect a welfare check upon arrival. Believe it or not, Mr. Zedda even started the first public waterworks company for Rock Hill. Mr. Zedda is what America is all about: Immigrants who come to the United States for a fresh start who make good by making America better. Your Grandfather was an Immigrant from Sweden who worked his entire life to make life in America better for his children and grandchildren. It is usually the second and third generations who really reap the benefit of America's freedoms and economic opportunities. Our forefathers have laid the foundation for success and happiness; following generations build the new buildings and grow society. This is why America must never stop Legal Immigration, which is what separates our Country from most others in the world. New people added to the "Stew in the Immigrant Melting Pot" is how America keeps the recipe of innovation and vitality percolating. Immigrants seeking a fresh start in a Country where men and women are judged by brains, brawn, and a willingness to sacrifice today for a better tomorrow will always make this Country great and young at the same time."**

⌘ ⌘ ⌘

By now I am sure you have figured out that my friend Jane White is a really good-looking girl. She has a twin sister, Jean, but they are not identical. When God made Jane, apparently he believed one gorgeous sister was enough. With beautiful blue eyes, freckles, and long blonde hair, she has a sexy smile that is inviting to almost every male. Jane also has beautiful boobs that will guarantee sweet dreams to any eighth grade boy.

While it is good to have a classmate like Jane, it's more rewarding to have her as your Girlfriend. The guys all say she is off limits because her dates are only with older guys. In fact, Bones said one time "he heard Jane had once dated an old man of 20!" I did ask her one time to go to a movie with me. Much to my surprise, Jane said, "Yes." Believe it or not, my Mom said, "OK." The movie we were going to see was "*Shane*" starring Alan Ladd. In the previews, we learned it was a Western that took place in Wyoming in the 1880's. We both liked how "*Shane*" stood up for the Homesteaders against the Cattlemen's hired gun played by Jack Palance, an Actor who my Dad said had been in the United States Air Force during World War II. I smiled when Jane said she thought the homesteader's young boy, "Joey," was cute and would be very handsome when he was older. I swear, Jane really notices the good-looking guys!

Jane and I always sit next to each other during band class. Actually, Jane sits between Terry Bones and me. Bones is a good buddy but like me he is a lousy clarinet player. The way he acts though you would think he was Benny Goodman. He says his mistakes are caused by the clarinet he "borrowed." It is owned by a seventh grade girl who rented it to Bones. His folks couldn't afford to buy him an instrument so he "rented" on the installment plan: "nothing down, the rest when you catch up with me," as he says.

My Mother drove me over to Jane's house to pick her up for our date. Mom had already called Jane's Mother to make sure the date met with her Mother's approval and to reassure her Family the date would be chaperoned. She also told me, "Be on your best behavior. Don't spit, use your handkerchief if you must sneeze, and, for goodness sake, don't break wind out loud." I asked her how I was supposed to fart quietly. She told me, "Don't be a Smartmouth, Mr. Jim, or your date will be over before it starts!" That was another thing, too: "Be a Gentleman!"

Jane and Jean, their Mom and Dad, and their brother, Goofy, met us at the door. I'm not lying; Goofy is what the whole Family calls him. I guess he earned the name because at ten years old he still messes his pants and wets the bed nightly. Jane says he needs an operation of some kind and the Rock Hill Lions Club plans to pay for the operation at the Morton Hospital soon.

Once in the house, everybody acted like we had been friends forever. Jane's Mom said, "It is real nice to have a Gentleman and his Mother ask for our daughter's companionship at the front door." Her Dad said, "Yes, I am tired of Jane bailing out the bedroom window to meet her beaus." He laughed when he said it, but I noticed Mom raised her eyebrows. Jane's Mother told her Dad to "stuff it" while Jane just smiled. We said good-bye, and her Parents told us to have a good time. Jane grabbed my hand, and out the door we went.

I started for the front door of the car, but Jane motioned for the back seat. By the time Mom was underneath the steering wheel, we were well seated behind her. I saw Mom start to say something, but then she only adjusted the rearview mirror.

Jane quickly let me know she was my girl that night when she took my hand to place it on her knee. My Mother told Jane to make sure I treated her like a gentleman should. Jane said if I didn't, she'd slug me really hard. Mom laughed. With that, Jane placed my hand on her lap. I swear I thought I could feel hair, let alone what we guys call the "Jaws of Life." Mom put the car in gear, and down the street we went. All too soon we were at the Z Theater. I never thought I'd ever complain about Mom driving too fast. She dropped us off and told us to be careful, watch out for each other, and she would return at 9:30 p.m. to pick us up when the movie ended.

In the lobby I bought one bag of popcorn and two paper cups of Coca-Cola from Harry, who was really surprised to see me on a date with Jane. Then Jane dragged me up the side stairs to the balcony seats. They were mostly filled by High School lovebirds. Normally, I sat about halfway down on the main floor with the guys. As we walked to our seats, a couple of older boys whistled at Jane. One fellow hollered for her to come over and sit on his lap. I ignored the comments and kept heading to my seat. Jane never said a word either; she just stuck out her tongue at the guy and then laughed.

We found seats in the front row that Jane wanted because she said she liked to put her feet up on the rail. As the movie started, the noise and commotion stopped. We first watched the previews, newsreel, cartoon, and then the feature started. When Alan Ladd appeared on the screen, the High School boys shouted, whistled, and stomped their feet. Ike, the Projectionist, flashed a "Quiet please" sign on the screen, and the High School boys erupted even louder.

Quickly, I was in pure heaven: sharing a bag of popcorn, drinking Coca-Cola, and holding Jane's hand. It was my first real date. I'll never forget when Jane told me to put my arm around her. I had been wondering if I should attempt such a move. But as quick as she could say do it now, around her shoulder my arm went. Boy, was it fun!

The only troubling thing was my hammer. I was afraid she was going to accidentally feel it. I didn't want her to think there was only one thing on my mind, and believe me, it wasn't Alan Ladd. In fact, I sat there wishing I had taped my hammer to my leg to keep it under control. When I told the guys later what I thought, they all said "baloney." They explained "the tremendous force of your hammer expanding would have just shattered the tape, creating an explosion that would have sounded like a submarine breaking apart deep in the ocean."

Somewhere during the movie when Alan Ladd was fighting Jack Palance, I had my first kiss. I couldn't believe how quickly it happened. All of a sudden, Jane turned to me and said, "Kiss me big guy." I puckered my lips and she swallowed me whole. Boy was it super! I can still taste her lipstick! I also swear I thought she purposely put her hand on my hammer. I tried to suck it back, but I'm afraid Big Elmer was standing at attention waiting for Jane to notice. Believe me Jane did! She said, "Not too bad for a little guy." I thought I felt my shorts getting wet. Jane must have kissed me three or four times during the movie. Each time I started to think about kissing her, darn if she didn't turn to kiss me first. It was almost like we had mental telepathy. I know my hammer did. I kept trying to tell Big Elmer to lie low, but he kept telling me to mind my own business. Jane just kept "accidentally" feeling his head when she reached for the popcorn. It was mighty embarrassing, but I have to admit it also felt pretty good.

When Alan Ladd as Shane rode away, the movie ended and the Z Theater lights came on. I thought the movie could have lasted forever. I certainly wished it had been a double feature. Unfortunately, all good things must end too soon, especially when a guy is on his first date. We rose from our seats and I gave Big Elmer a whack with the back of my hand to make him relax. Jane smiled almost like she knew what I was doing and we started toward the balcony stairs. As we passed a couple of Rock Hill High School students, one guy said, "Hey big fellow did you cop yourself a feel during the movie?" I must have looked bewildered because I truly was not sure what he meant. Jane knew though, because she glared at the guy and said, "Why don't you just jam it in your big mouth Barker!" She squeezed my hand and down the stairs we bounded.

Mom was parked right in front of the Z Theater when we walked into the street. Mom motioned for us to sit up front with her, much to our regret. As we drove away, she asked if we enjoyed the movie. We said. "Yes!" She noticed Jane was holding my hand deep in her lap and lipstick smudges were on my face. Other than look surprised, she never made a comment. Once I had walked Jane to her door and we were on our way home Mom said, "Listen, Mr. Loverboy, Jane White is much too old for you. It'll be a while before you enjoy a repeat performance of that kind of entertainment!" And dog-gone-it, it was, too!

⌘ ⌘ ⌘

One day in the spring, all of the boys in the seventh and eighth grades were directed by Mr. Don to report to the Library for a special meeting. We had no idea what to expect though we were very excited and curious.

Mr. Don introduced Mr. Ben Tanner, who some of us had as a Teacher in the sixth grade. He was much loved by all of the boys and girls in the entire school. We could not wait to hear what Mr. Tanner had to say.

Mr. Tanner at fifty-five was one of the oldest Teachers in the Rock Hill School District. He was over six feet tall, weighed two hundred pounds and stood ramrod straight. He was known as: "A man's man." At eighteen years of age, Mr. Tanner had served as a Doughboy in World War I in Europe. After the war during the 1920's and 1930's, he served in the Washington National Guard. Then at the age of forty-five he was ordered to report for active duty during World War II. He eventually served in Europe on the March to Berlin as a Sergeant Major in the US Army Infantry. Mr. Tanner has a deep voice and a serious manner. When he speaks all students, girls as well as boys, listen intently. We boys truly could not wait to hear his message. In Rock Hill there was no other person we respected more.

"Fellows," Mr. Tanner began, "Shakespeare said, 'A rose by any other name smells just as sweet.' Today I am going to talk to you about your future. I am going to talk about sex. Yes, that is right. S - E - X. There are certain words I can not use, but I will substitute those words with others that I know you will understand. I have followed the educational and athletic progress of most of you fellows. I want you to know that I am very impressed with your development. I believe that your group of boys has a bright future ahead of you, if you mind your business and concentrate on improving your God-given brains and athletic talent.

"Now, to the subject of the moment: You fellows are reaching an age in which you are becoming young men. Women or girls are suddenly an important part of your daily social life. Parts of your body such as your hammer are starting to cause certain feelings that you have never had before. The smell of a girl strikes you differently. You get breathless more quickly. You have different dreams at night, some of them wet. Listen, guys, you are not the first or the only fellows who have gone through these changes. I have, Mr. Don has, your Dads have. What is important is that you manage these feelings. You must get through this crucial period without making a mistake that will adversely affect you for the rest of your life.

Rock Hill

"Rock Hill, your Teachers, and your Parents expect big things from your group of boys. Because Mr. Don and I have spent years developing men, we know of your great potential for success. We also know of the pitfalls that can stop any one of you from reaching the heights of accomplishment. Fellows, bluntly, you must learn how to keep your God-given sexual urges under control. Now I know the girls in your class are a group of good--looking girls. I also know that just by nature the girls will be naturally more interested in sex than you are. You may not believe this statement but, believe me, it is true at this time: girls are just more mature than you are at this age.

"You men have the brains and character traits required to accomplish any goal you wish to set for yourself. You just have to continue to study hard and practice with a determination to succeed no matter the challenge or cost. Controlling your sexual desires will not be easy. Why? Because an important part of a man is simply being a man. God made man one half of what is required in the procreation process. All too soon men and women, boys and girls, find that having sex is not only for continuing the species, it is also damn fine fun. Now, God meant it to be fun, never doubt it. Why, guys, there is nothing better than having sex with someone you deeply love and wish to spend the rest of your life with. But the time has to be right.

"Men, there is nothing, I repeat nothing, sadder than a boy and girl having a baby before they both have finished their education. You must wait until you are launched in a career and able to support a Family. At your age you must understand that when you satisfy the urge to make love to a girl, you may be ending your chance to go to College or the Military where you can continue your education. Getting a girl pregnant is an act that Mr. Don and I would not wish on any one of you at your age. Please believe me when I say it is an easy thing to do when you are young and filled with such fertile juices. Now, I understand that most of you have yet to date or even hold a girl's hand, especially you thirteen- and fourteen-year-old fellows. There is no doubt that some people in Rock Hill may think my little talk today is unnecessary. My my, you are all too young to hear about such behavior! Well believe me gentlemen, especially you older fifteen-year-old guys, Miss Temptation will arouse your interest one of these days soon. When she does, you must be prepared to handle such an alluring visitor.

"Now, there is nothing wrong with holding hands or a few kisses. However, the challenge comes when the act of petting starts. Touch a boob here — touch a boob there. A caress in the crotch area. That is when, my good men, you have to apply the brakes! Guys, you have no idea how easy it is to cross the "Bridge of No Return." God made all of us with free will. It is up to you to resist your natural urges until you are well educated and ready for a mature relationship with a woman.

"Fellows listen to me please. Let me assure you that if you have to date Mrs. Palmer or one of her Five Daughters — and you know what I mean, I know - to relieve the pressure of desire, do not worry one moment about such an act. That is much better than ruining your young life and that of a pretty

Rock Hill

girlfriend. Another thing, if some idiot ever suggests that dating Mrs. Palmer will make you go crazy, let me assure you, - THAT individual is off his rocker. If dating Mrs. Palmer will make you go crazy, then half the world's population is crazy. Also, the next time some religious nut tries to put the fear of the devil in you or threatens you with the depths of hell for dating Mrs. Palmer, just ignore such foolishness. That person is truly out of his mind!

"I am certain that some of you boys think condoms are the absolute answer for birth control. More than one unhappy young Father thought the same thing. For your information, they are not just used for birth control. Uncle Sam provided Doughboys like me during World War I with condoms to prevent venereal disease—A disease I hope you never catch. I also know that some of you guys think it is smart to carry a condom in your billfold. Guys, that little circular ridge is a sure give - away of your ignorance. My advice is for you to show maturity by throwing away that condom today. Do not even think about having sex with a girl now. Believe me, there is no such thing as safe sex at your age.

"Fellows, why are Mr. Don and I taking the time to talk with you about the subject of sex, girlfriends, and babies? It is simple, men: it is because we care about your future. I wish someone had taken me by the neck and sat me down and said these things when I was your age. You boys really don't know a great deal about me. Oh sure, you have heard about my time in the Military. I had some of you in my sixth grade class where you learned some of my history. Let me tell you more.

"Guys, I came from a very poor Family in Kentucky. I lived on a farm that my Daddy gave his health for —so he could raise me and my seven brothers and sisters. That number does not count the three who died from illness. My Mother worked from dawn to dusk and sometimes half the night when there was sickness in the Family. Life was hard, hard, hard. Life was especially hard for women who bore the brunt of childbirth. Do not think for one minute that every Mother wanted a large family or looked forward to being pregnant again. I swore growing up, as I helped my Dad in the tobacco fields, that I was going to get myself a College Education. I was not going to make a living killing myself at the end of a mule and a plow. I very much wanted a wife and children when the time was right. Also, I intended to take good care of my Family with a career with some fine company.

"But guess what? I became a Father at the young age of sixteen. Yes, I know it is hard to believe. Boys, it can happen so easily when you let your emotions run away with your brains. What happened to me then? Well the first thing that happened was I HAD to marry the girl. Then I was forced out of school and HAD to take a job in a local sawmill to put food on the table. If you think it was easy to give up my education, think again. It was NOT. If you think at that age it was easy to provide for a Family and be an adequate husband and a Father, it was NOT! Two years later, as sometimes happens in life, the baby got sick with Whooping Cough and died. My wife and I decided the best thing for both of us was to get a

Rock Hill

divorce and start fresh again, which we did. She went her way and I went mine.

"At the age of nineteen when World War I came along, I volunteered to be a member of Uncle Sam's finest, The U.S. Army. Upon my return from Europe, since I was too old for High School, I took an entrance exam at a local State Teachers College. I passed my exams and started College in 1920. I graduated in 1925 and I have been teaching ever since, except for my US Army service during World War II.

"Fellows, here at Rock Hill School we are blessed with very few groups of boys and girls such as yours. You boys are smart, teachable, hardworking, and good looking, and do not think for one minute that looks are not important in life - - They are. Finally, you have that rare quality that Teachers adore but seldom discover in so many members of a single class: a burning desire and steadfast determination to succeed in life. I can say the same for most of the girls in your class. They will be challenged soon, too. Their challenge will be to say "NO" to older boys. In the heat of passion, I fear, some may make a mistake. A girl may give in just to shut a man up, the consequences of which she may regret for the rest of her life.

"Now you fellows should know that women in the future will have opportunities in the workplace that women of today do not. Fellows, our Country is changing to give women the opportunity to be full-fledged members of our workplace. I predict women will soon be permitted by society to fill any job in this Country. Remember, women successfully replaced men in the workplace during World War II when so many men were fighting Overseas. For their hard work, I salute "Rosie the Riveter" and the other women who manufactured the War Supplies we needed to wage war against the Germans and the Japanese. To compete successfully in the workplace in the future, I predict your generation of men will have to get either a College Education or Trade School Training.

"Men, in Rock Hill there are few employment opportunities if you drop out of school to raise a young Family. We have two industries: logging and sawmills. Both of these occupations come with hard dangerous physical work. Most companies have no health benefits, no retirement other than Social Security, and few opportunities to better oneself through promotion. It is true we do have a few dairy and blueberry farms, but your best bet there is to marry the farmer's daughter. Unfortunately, in most cases, the farmer's daughter already has a husband. We have no manufacturing plants in Rock Hill. Unless your Father owns a business, your chance of remaining here in Rock Hill to make a living is slim to none.

"Elsewhere, you are going to have the world to explore for employment opportunities. But first, men, you have to get prepared by getting a College education or Trade School Training. Some of you may choose the Military for a career, and what a damn fine career it is. In any case, it is almost a surety that you will be leaving Rock Hill after High School Graduation. It is guaranteed that the best way to go on with your life is to proceed without the expensive baggage of a

Rock Hill

wife and child that you cannot afford and truly do not want or need at this time.

"During College, I met a beautiful, wonderful woman. After we both graduated and had started teaching careers, we married and have been together for over twenty-five years. We have four beautiful children who we have been able to raise on a Teacher's salary. I have had an outstanding career and a very satisfying marriage, both founded on love. There is nothing — I repeat nothing — that brings a man more satisfaction than being at ease with his financial state in life, while loving his wife and what he does for a living.

"Again, I want each of you to know Mr. Don and I have very high expectations for this class. You men are excellent athletes, proven scholars, and damn hard workers. You come from outstanding Families who are very proud of your accomplishments and provide you with great support. Now, most of you know of my integrity, I would not make these statements if I did not believe them. Your class of boys and girls is remarkable. If you boys keep your hammer in your pockets and always use your brains to think with, each of you will travel a long way on the road to a successful life.

"I want you to listen very carefully to me now. Most of you know about my Military background. I wish to speak especially to the boys who pride themselves on being athletes. US Army General Douglas MacArthur, who was Commandant of West Point at the time, said, 'On the athletic fields of today are the men who will be our country's leaders on the battlefields of tomorrow.' I have fought in two World

Wars with each being 'The One to End all Wars.' Gentlemen, unfortunately there will always be Wars and Armies to fight them. Some day your turn will come. When it does, I pray you will answer your Nation's call with courage and a willingness to sacrifice for others. If you pay the ultimate sacrifice, Death on the Battlefield, I pray you will be a hero, not a coward. I believe you boys have the stuff it takes to conquer your fears and succeed in combat. There is nothing better than training to answer a man's doubt. Hell, at one time every member of the Military has had his doubts and fears, men! The confidence that comes with training and age will protect you. I deeply believe that when opportunity strikes, you will be more than ready to step up to the plate, take a healthy swing, and hit the ball out of the park.

"Right now, there is a War going on in Korea. Of course, the politicians are calling it a 'police action.' Remember what I said about Shakespeare and the rose? This is a good example men. It is not a 'police action.' It is a war, plain and simple: An undeclared war regardless of what the politicians wish to call it. Men are dying as I speak. Women and children too, I am sure. Your Country's Military is right in the thick of it – as perhaps we should be. Only our Nation's Leaders have all the facts. I just do not like our Leaders lying about it. I trust President Eisenhower, a great Military Leader if there ever was one, will either stop this total waste of manpower and treasure soon or fight the only kind of war this Country should ever fight: A war of total annihilation. Put the United States on total war status like we fought World War II, then, go out

Rock Hill

to get the job done and bring our brave military people home with a victory, not a damn stalemate or truce.

"General Douglas MacArthur has also said the United States should never — repeat NEVER — get into a land War in Asia. Believe me, the Great General has lived in Asia much of his life and he knows what he is talking about. Unfortunately I fear, sometime in the future the politicians in Washington, to either 'Kill Commies' or 'Stop Communistic ideas from taking over the World,' will ignore such advice and fight a huge and costly land war there anyway. One thing I do know for sure is the United States stands for Freedom, now and always. Some of you men someday will be required to help defend this Country and our Nation's Ideals. When called, square your shoulders, stand up straight and shout, 'Here, Sir. Ready, Sir.'

"I wish to remind you fellows that I had in the sixth grade of a statement I made at the time. I am certain most of you will remember my words. It will not hurt to hear them again, along with those of you who were not in my class. When it comes to people: 'Those who can —DO! Some who have DONE — eventually also TEACH.' I believe the best Teacher is one who has worked and proved himself competent elsewhere prior to attempting to teach young minds in the classroom. Some of you may think you would like to be a Teacher. In my opinion, many of you will make fine Teachers and Coaches. But, be a DOER first. Get experience outside the classroom first to improve the skills and knowledge that you will bring to your students.

"A man can accomplish generally anything he sets his mind to do. Just as long as that man is willing to pay the price for the training and knowledge required to succeed at the task. Indeed, once you're prepared, life can be a thrilling, exciting trip with experiences of unbelievable challenge. Just be willing to volunteer to be a candidate when the opportunities arise.

"In my case, I chose the Military for physical and mental challenges. While serving my Country, I put my life on the line to join other Americans to keep our Country safe and preserve our Nation's Great Freedoms. There is no greater joy men, than to be able to stand tall and say, 'I did my share when Uncle Sam called.'

"After returning from War, I realized I could also help my Country by teaching young people Reading, Writing, Mathematics, and Science. I soon learned my life outside a classroom had helped me gain the respect of my students in the classroom which in turn, helped make me a better Teacher. In short, my Military Experiences and College Education allowed me to combine wisdom with knowledge to teach with greater success and personal satisfaction.

"In conclusion, please listen now to a very important subject dear to my heart. I want to talk to you now about a FORCE that someday, somewhere, you are going to need to help you stay alive while enduring a challenge that could be unexpected and life threatening. That ever present Force is the Power of Prayer. Whether you believe it or not, there is a Supreme Being that made your body, mind and this earth that you know as home. You may always contact that Supreme Being through

Prayer. Now, I am not talking about Organized Religion and I am not knocking Organized Religion either. I do not care if you are Christian, Jewish, or Muslim — a religion that most of you have probably never heard of. Organized Religion may have a place in your life, if you choose. As a matter of fact, Organized Religion has been a blessing for America in particular and the world in general. Indeed, The United States was founded on Judeo-Christian principles. Organized Religion, however, has also been the root cause of many wars in the past. It will be in the future; some you may have to fight in.

"I must add that one of the most despicable acts by one Religion against another was the horrible treatment of the Jews during World War II by the Germans, a Christian nation. Don't ever let anyone tell you the German Concentration Camps did not exist. I was there. I saw them: A terrible example of man's inhumanity to another man. I pray it never happens again. But, because there is evil on this earth, and you are going to know it in time, it surely will. I also pray that you boys will do your best to stop it.

"One man's Religion is his business. We should not care one bit in what Church, Synagogue or Mosque a man worships — just as long as one man's belief does not infringe on another.

"No, I am not talking about Organized Religion. I am talking now about connecting that Life Spirit that exists in your body and mind with the Supreme Being, or God. When the problem is bigger than you are, close your eyes and open your mind. Then, have a private talk with God or the Supreme Being or whatever you wish to call the Higher Power. Tell

JUNIOR HIGH

Him of your need, your hurts, your challenges. Believe me, He always listens. Does he always answer? YES! It's just that sometimes we mortals do not like the answers we get. But believe me, God does know best! He does answer our Prayers —ALWAYS! In a foxhole, hospital room, or a city park when the need is bigger than you are: Pray, Men, Pray.

"In closing, there is an old saying, **'When you grow old, the only things you regret are the risks you didn't take.' Well, I will give you one better.** *"The Risks You Take Are The Things You Most Remember When You Grow Old.'* Get prepared, men! If you are willing to try, life will throw all kinds of pitches of opportunity at you. Get prepared to hit them out of the park! Mr. Don and I have no doubt that with perseverance; you will succeed beyond your wildest dreams. Thank you and good day. You may now return to your home rooms."

That night I told Dad and Mom what Mr. Tanner had to say. Dad said, "Good for Old Tanner. What he said Jim, needed to be said. I hope you take it to heart. Mr. Tanner has been through a great deal in his life. He knows what he is talking about. I just hope the female Teachers are passing on the same information to the girls." Mom said, "Jim, Mr. Tanner is right. You have your whole life ahead of you. You have lots of time to chase the girls. In the future, I will not interfere with your afternoon naps with Pug."

Dad glanced at Mom and me with a curious look on his face. I knew then Mom had not told on me. I said to myself, "Thanks Mom." Mom continued to say, "As for the girls, you really do Jim, have a beautiful class of girls. But I don't think

173

Rock Hill

they will have much to worry about with you boys. It is the older fellows who will be the ones they have to deny. As far as the lovely Miss Jane White, it will be a long time before you again enjoy her charms by taking her to another movie. Mr. Tanner is also right about Prayer, Jim. But then, you have had a head start on its use through your Faith. Just be assured, it is the most Powerful Force available to you, or anyone."

⌘ ⌘ ⌘

Annually during the last week of May, the entire school salutes the community of Rock Hill for their support throughout the year with a pageant called "Community Day." This year the main feature was a play about Johnny Appleseed with yours truly as Johnny, wearing his well known Tin Pot Hat! Mrs. Downs suggested I check out several books from the School Library to study Johnny's life. I was surprised to learn his Dad had served with George Washington in the Continental Army during the American Revolutionary War. Johnny Appleseed was born in Massachusetts in 1774 and died in 1845 in Indiana. During his lifetime, Johnny planted nurseries filled with apple trees in Pennsylvania, Ohio, Indiana, Illinois, and West Virginia. We have many apple orchards in Eastern Washington. In fact, Wenatchee is called: "The Apple Capital Of The World." I honor Johnny Appleseed by trying to*:* " *Eat An Apple A Day — To Keep The Doctor Away.* "

Johnny Appleseed was also a man of God, preaching the Gospel to Whites and Indians alike. It was said the Native

JUNIOR HIGH

Americans thought he was a gentle man touched by the Great Spirit; even Indian Tribes on the warpath left him alone. Another aspect of his life that meant a lot to me was his love for animals. Johnny said they were a gift from God and should be respected and revered. I know exactly how he felt because I have a pet skunk that I named Chynel for the famous perfume that my Dad gave Mom for Christmas one year. I agree with Johnny Appleseed that God's creatures can make a man love and cherish them. I love Chynel and always will. More than she will ever know.

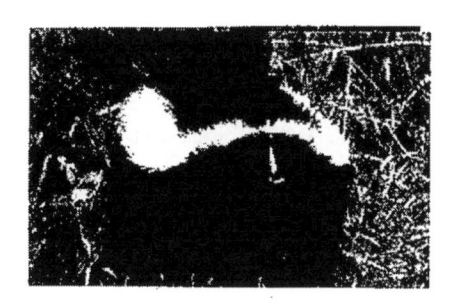

Chynel, Gone but not forgotten. I shall always love her!

Rock Hill

    Another big feature of Community Day is the Rock Hill High School Senior Girls Maypole Dance. Jane White says, "Every girl in school dreams of some day dancing in the Maypole Dance." This spectacle features a tall pole that has colorful ribbons hanging from the top. The pole is placed by Ag students on the High School lawn. The Senior Girls are dressed in beautiful formal gowns. During the program, each girl holds the end of a ribbon and dance/walks to the music of a recorded symphony. As the girls dance around the Maypole, the ribbons are wound around and down to the bottom of the pole. Believe me, it is a gorgeous part of Community Day. Everyone in Rock Hills loves to watch the girls in this beautiful and memorable dance. My Mom said, "This graceful dance is a testament to the beauty and wholesomeness of our young women in Rock Hill." Dad said, "Some of the girls in the dance are almost as pretty as your Mom." Mom just smiled at Dad, but I could tell she truly appreciated the comment.

    Dad and Mom told me the story of how the Maypole Dance came to Community Day. It seems the aristocracy of Rock Hill, the Hurley Family - - Mr. Cecil, Mr. Clarence and Mr. Percy, the Mayor of Rock Hill - - brought the Maypole Dance with them when their Father immigrated to America from the British Isles. Since the Hurleys are a most distinguished family with farms and businesses in the area, and since Clarence Hurley sits on the Rock Hill District School Board, the school thought it would honor the Hurley's contribution to our way of life by adding the beautiful Maypole feature to the Community Day Festivities. Because the Hurley Family has financially helped many Rock Hill citizens start their own companies (such as my Dad, Uncle Alvin and Uncle Sandy), Respect and Appreciation were always due the Hurleys.

In an indirect way you might say I am related to the Hurley Clan, too: Cousin Harold married Jean Hurley, the beautiful daughter of Mr. and Mrs. Percy Hurley. The Hurleys I know fairly well are the sons and daughters of the three brothers: Cecil, Clarence and Percy. They are: Barbara, Beverly, Dick, Jean, Norma, Roger and Steve.

Dad said the boys were all super athletes and Mom said the girls were some of the loveliest in Rock Hill.

Roger is half owner of a Gypo Logging Outfit. His partner is Glen Ozzy who with his wife Laura play and sing at most of the funerals in Rock Hill. Boy, you should hear their rendition of "The Old Rugged Cross". Laura sings while Glen plays a "Crying Mandolin." Mom says it reminds her of funerals back in the Ozarks when she was a young girl. Roger is also a good friend of my Flying Buddy Mac, the Log Truck Driver. You ought to see Roger's wife, Imogene! What a Beauty! She's the Daughter of Mr. and Mrs. Mc Clutchens, a very kind couple from the State of Nebraska. I mow their lawn and Mrs. Mc Clutchens always gives me a nice, big tip and usually a piece of homemade cake, too! Roger's Brother Dick is a Flying "A" Fuel Distributor and delivers diesel fuel to logging companies in the area. Dick's wife Betty is a knockout, too.

Dad and Mom also said that the Hurleys were well known throughout Rock Hill for practicing and teaching others by their example of how to live your life - - by **"The Golden Rule"**:

"Do Unto Others As You Would Have Them Do Unto You."

When Community Day and my Johnny Appleseed act was over, Mr. Don said to me, "You should consider a career in show business." When I told Sam Wilcox what Mr. Don had said, Sam remarked, "Yea, you'd make a good replacement for Elmer Fudd."

⌘ ⌘ ⌘

Soon I hope to take flying lessons. The law says the minimum age to obtain a Private Pilot License or fly solo is sixteen. Actually, I've already had some instruction from a local Pilot who owns a Taylorcraft BC-12. It is a two-seat side – by - side airplane with a wheel instead of a stick to operate the ailerons on the wings and the elevator portion of the tail. The owner of the Airplane is Bing Johnson, a World War II Lockheed P – 38 Pilot who is a good-sized guy with a silly sense of humor. He's always telling me about some new joke he's heard. Like did I hear about the blonde that backed into a propeller — dis-as-ter!

Bing works in a sawmill and flies now just for fun. He said I'd make a great pilot because I have a soft touch and really love to fly. He says these are two very important keys to being an outstanding Pilot.

Bing says he still loves to fly, but after "Dog Fighting" the Nips, for him flying now is always going to be for fun. He says killing people changes one's perspective in life. In war some people deserve to die but unfortunately, the innocent too often get killed with the guilty.

The small grass strip west of town is fairly quiet now. The BC-12 is the only aircraft kept at the field. Will Stone moved to Alaska to fly in the bush as a Commercial Pilot. The inactivity is quite a change from just after the war. Bing told me that people move on with their dreams, change toys, or have to spend their money on their Families in other ways. He says he's lucky he never married. Being a bachelor, he always gets to do what HE WANTS! However, he admits there was a time when he would have given his extra flight suit for a Female Copilot who could keep the airplane in proper trim and tighten the nuts on the Pilot at the end of the flight!

Bing lets me wash the Taylorcraft and help with refueling. The BC-12 has a twelve-gallon tank right in front of the windshield behind the engine. To keep track of the amount of gas in the tank, a metal wire sticks through a small hole in the filler cap to show content. We keep gasoline in five-gallon steel cans. To clean the fuel, we strain the gas through a chamois. Dirty fuel can plug a carburetor, stopping the engine—not a good thing to have happen when you're airborne and wish to stay aloft.

With Bing at my side, I've taken the Taylorcraft off and landed the ship by myself. Once in the air, it's easy to fly a plane. In fact, as Bing says, if the ship is properly trimmed, it'll fly itself if the Pilot will just keep out of the way. Turns are a bit tricky. The Pilot has to kick in the proper amount of rudder with the foot pedals to position the rudder properly.

The airplane will then track the circumference of a circle precisely. The right amount of coordination between the feet on the rudder pedals and the hands on the wheel to move the ailerons, elevator, and rudder in harmony together is the goal. Turning the wheel to the left will cause the left aileron, the movable portion of the trailing edge of the wing, to rise and the right aileron to lower. Increased air pressure under the right wing and, at the same time, decreased air pressure under the left wing will occur. The end result is a lifting of the right wing around the horizontal axis. With proper left rudder pedal pressure at the same time, you can make a perfect left turn. Just the opposite, of course, for a right turn.

While flying over Rock Hill Valley, Bing told me, "An airplane in flight sits on a point of equilibrium. A Pilot operating the wheel or stick in conjunction with the rudder pedals, if he's worth his salt, can maintain equilibrium even in level, climbing, or descending turns. A lack of proper coordination causes an airplane to skid or slip around a turn, making for an uncomfortable and potentially dangerous flight. A sloppy Pilot is a poor and hazardous Pilot. When an airplane stalls, the wings lose lift and it can literally fall from the sky. Jim, more than one guy has lost his life by stalling out close to the ground while turning." He's always on my case about not using enough or too much rudder pedal in a turn.

We practice stalls when we reach a couple thousand feet in the air. It's fun. It's like riding on a roller coaster. Up, up, up, nose up. When the aircraft slows down, it seems like you're just hanging on thin air. The engine is quiet because the throttle has been reduced to idle. Back, back, back, you pull the wheel into your chest — then, over the plane goes. All of a sudden you're looking straight down. The ground looks like it's coming right at you. To recover, you add engine power while pushing the wheel forward and neutralizing the rudder pedals to point the airplane straight ahead. A Pilot has to be very watchful when returning to level flight. Carefully you must add cruise power. In stall mode, improper pressure right or left on the rudder pedals can cause an airplane to enter a tailspin. More than one Pilot has not lived to brag about practicing stalls too close to the ground. Unfortunately, sometimes, neither have his passengers.

Because an airplane has to be stalled just prior to landing, Bing has me practice stalls all the time. Bing says, "When an airplane stalls, it means the airplane has lost the necessary lift to stay airborne. Gravity has taken over. And, whether it's the Taylorcraft BC-12 or a Douglas DC-7 Airliner, a well executed stall just prior to touchdown should always equal a soft, beautiful landing." He did add, "Yes, it is true that sometimes due to a short runway length, hazardous weather conditions, or aircraft Type or Weight some Pilots will "Fly" an aircraft onto the runway surface; more often than not, such a touchdown only happens when flight experience tells the Captain a second attempt at landing, called a 'Missed Approach,' may be necessary." Bing added, "You must always remember, Jim, that "Old Man Fate" is always lurking over a Pilot's shoulder, waiting for him to make a foolish decision at the wrong time in the wrong place. When "Old Man Fate" intervenes, and it does happen occasionally even to very experience Pilots, the result can be an unnecessary catastrophe with a loss of Passengers, Pilots, and Airplanes."

Once in a while Bing and I fly to the Toledo Airport. It's like flying to a different world. Stationed beside a five-thousand-foot asphalt runway is a CAA Flight Service Station. During World War II, the Toledo field was an emergency and training airport located about halfway between Portland and Seattle. Today, US Government Employees take hourly weather reports and provide radio service to arriving, departing, and cross-country Pilots.

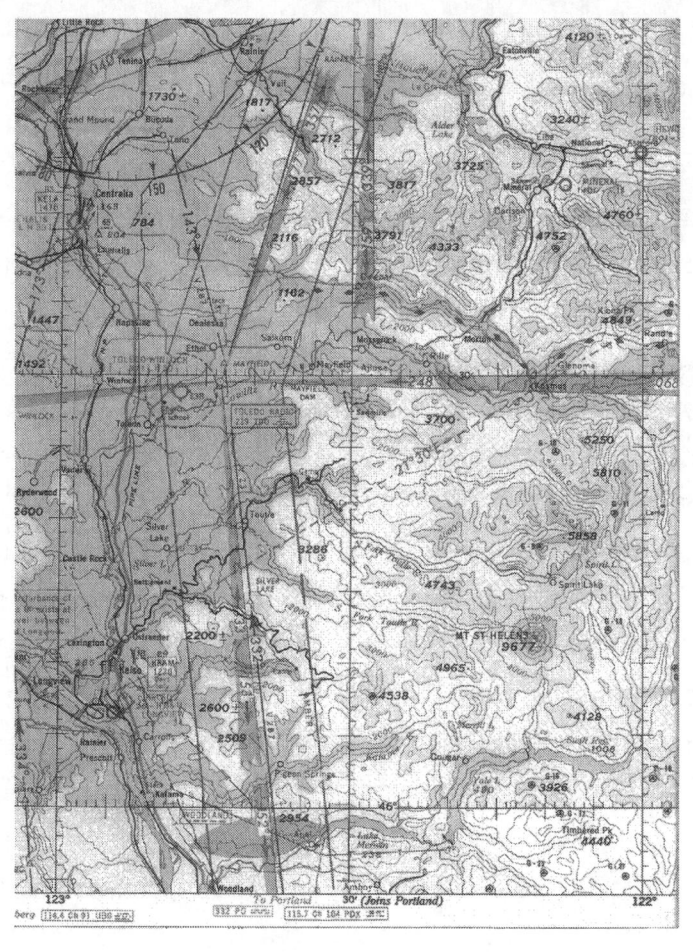

Toledo Airfield can sometimes be tricky to use because a prevailing crosswind is almost always blowing over the runway. A guy has to always be alert, or a ground loop or something worse will announce your arrival.

Bing always banters with the US Government Employees about not working for a living. They tease him about being an over-the-hill World War II US Army Bomber Pilot with a desire to return to the day when everyone called him "Sir." It's all good- natured. He says the job they do is underappreciated. Most Pilots don't realize how valuable the CAA Flight Service Station is until bad weather strikes or people make foolish flight decisions.

Since Toledo has self-service gasoline for sale, we top the tank. We also have a bottle of pop and a candy bar. Bing says it's better to always fly with a full stomach in the Pilot as well as a full fuel tank in the airplane. A Pilot can navigate the bumps on the road in the sky a little easier and extra gasoline equals an extra margin of safety if a Pilot is temporarily lost on the way home. This can happen to even the best Pilots when flying by *"PILOTAGE"*, the practice of looking out the window and recognizing landmarks on the ground to navigate.

For me, an airport at night has always been an inviting place. The atmosphere invokes mystery, travel, and adventure. Sometimes on the way back home from Grandpa's house late on Sunday nights, we drive by the Toledo Emergency Airport. I really like to see the landing field lit up. I also like to watch the white and green rotating beacon that throws flashes of light into the sky. They help lead VFR (Visual Flight Rule) Pilots to the airfield when it is dark or stormy. In my mind, the airport beacon is a light signal that reaches out to touch Pilots throughout the night sky, linking them to the field by an electrical tether. I imagine the rotating lights are saying, "Fly away bold Pilots but remember, my rotating green and white flashing lights are always here to help guide you safely home."

I sure hope some day to fly in the Military or have my own plane, and encourage others to enjoy flying as well. Some of the finest people I've met so far have been involved in Aviation. I hope I can say I'm still flying when I'm ninety-nine years old!

⌘ ⌘ ⌘

Call Me Lucky
"An airplane is like a good woman: Treat her with respect and she is yours for the asking; Treat her with indifference and she may never forgive you." This statement was attached to the Instrument Panel of Jim's Commonwealth SkyRanger - "Call Me Lucky."

I do have to admit that when I am not thinking about airplanes or flying, my mind is on Baseball in the summertime. At Rock Hill we have a Babe Ruth team. I play left field and am a pretty good hitter. I get on base and score a lot of runs. I don't hit many extra base hits, mostly singles and a few solid doubles once in a while. Because I run the bases awfully fast, I can turn a single into a double thanks to hustle. Since I am just five feet and one inch tall, I also walk a lot because I have a pretty small strike zone. I steal a lot of bases, too. That's because I am so quick. I usually get a pretty good lead. The pitcher has a hard time holding me close to the bag. Sometimes when he throws to first base to pick me off, I just head for second instead.

Because I'm so good at getting on base, I'm always the first one in the lineup to bat. I have always been proud of my position in the batting lineup. Billy Houser bats second and plays shortstop. He's a good hitter and has a great throwing arm. Roy Silver bats third and plays third base. Roy had polio when he was young and it's a miracle to see how well he has recovered. My good friend, Mason, bats cleanup and can hit the ball a mile. He plays centerfield and is awfully good at throwing the ball fast and accurately from deep in the outfield.

This Spring the four of us went to Portland, Oregon on the Union Pacific Train. Our primary purpose for the trip was to visit the Wilson Sporting Goods Regional Warehouse so that each of us could buy a bat. Our folks weren't sure about letting us go alone, but we convinced them there was safety in numbers.

My Mom drove us to the train depot in Chehalis for the two - hour trip to Portland. Upon arrival, we caught a taxi at the station for the trip to the Wilson Sporting Goods Warehouse. We asked the Taxi Driver if he had ever hauled any famous people. He said sure: "Bob Hope, Gary Cooper, Rita

Hayworth, Babe Ruth, and Mr. Edward Clark." We asked him who Edward Clark was. He said, "Glad you asked. Edward Clark is a Famous Oregon Dairy Farmer who had thirteen inches of 'Love Muscle.' This man had to keep his 'Love Muscle' wrapped around his leg just like it was an Amazon Python. He couldn't keep a wife, girl-friend, or a Holstein cow happy. They all either ran away or stopped giving milk. The Dairy Farmer was in town to have the University of Oregon School of Medicine Surgeons provide a solution. It all sounded pretty far-fetched to us, but it made for an interesting ride. We also asked him if anything else memorable ever happened to him while driving "the Hack". He said, "Damn betcha, boys!"

"One time I picked up a fare at Union Station," he continued. "The man got in the back seat and threw a hundred-dollar bill at me and said, 'Get me to the airport in twenty-five minutes and the change is all yours.'

"Well," the driver said, "I was all eyes up front watching traffic, running lights, and overall trying my best to earn that tip. I really wasn't paying attention to what was happening in the backseat.

"When I arrived at the airport just in the nick of time, my fare jumped out without a hello or a good-bye. He just vanished. I never thought much about it until I looked into the back seat on the floor. Yep, you guessed it. Damn if that guy hadn't taken a dump on the floor when I wasn't looking. Unbelievable, wasn't it?"

"What did you do then?" we asked in amazement.

"Well, I did the only thing an *"honest"* man could do. I went to the nearest police station and told them my story," he said.

"What did they say?" we asked.

"Well, the cops said for me to advertise in the *Portland Oregonian* for three days under lost and found classified. If nobody claimed the dump, then it was mine to keep!" We all laughed. The Taxi Driver let us out at the Front Door of the Wilson Sporting Goods Warehouse. We thanked him with the fare and a tip.

The people at Wilson Sporting Goods were very nice when we arrived. The manager met us and said that normally the store did not sell retail. Their customers were the sporting good stores where we shopped back home. But since we had come such a long way and were obviously important baseball players, this one time, he would make an exception. We could indeed each purchase one bat.

Boy was it something to see all the bats they stocked. It was almost unbelievable. I picked out a Johnny Mize model with a big thick handle. I always felt more comfortable at the plate with such a bat. The other guys selected their choices. The Receptionist who was very nice, called us a Taxi. When the Taxi Driver arrived, we found he was an old grump who didn't talk very much or even ask what we ballplayers were doing in town. Did we have a tournament or what? We made a point of only paying exactly what the meter said when the Taxi Driver delivered us back in the downtown area. No curiosity or entertainment equaled no tip, as far as we were concerned!

JUNIOR HIGH

Since we had a couple of hours to kill before the train left to return home, we decided to walk the streets in downtown Portland. As we walked, we swung our bats and joked with each other about games we had played. We talked about game winning hits and super catches. I'm sure the people walking by us thought we were genuine rubes. We didn't care because in our minds we were important visiting athletes in the City Of Roses.

Everybody said it was too bad the Portland Beavers of the Triple - A Pacific Coast League were not playing in town. We could have gone to a game. My favorite Beaver was Joe Brovia. He was a homerun hitter and played outfield just like me. But Joe could sure hit the horsehide a lot further.

Unfortunately for us, on that day the Beavers were playing the Hollywood Stars in Southern California. We really would have liked to see a game at Metropolitan Stadium. We also talked about visiting the *Portland Oregonian* to meet Mr. L. H. Gregory, their famous Sports Editor. He always writes about achievement in sports and the importance of using proper grammar when speaking or writing. We read his column every day. He writes like an English Professor, and it seems like he knows every famous player and Coach in every sport in the Country. In the end, we decided it was probably not possible to see the busy Sports Editor without a prior appointment.

One thing we did try to do was get into a Burlesque Theater. We walked by a place that had pictures of the current strippers out front. Boy, did they have big boobs! A lady named Tempest Storm was the headliner. She was sure pretty.

We stepped up to the ticket booth. In the window was a sign that read "Must be 18 years old." The old guy behind the window looked at us with a rather quizzical look and said, "ID please." We said we'd left them at home, and he said, "No ID, no tickets." So that was that. No boobs, no pretty faces, no Tempest Storm. Since it would soon be time to catch the afternoon train back to Chehalis, we returned to the Union Train Station. With our new bats, we were ready for the next game.

In the spring and early summer, we play our baseball games in the Babe Ruth League. In addition to players from Rock Hill, teams are from throughout Lewis County. At the conclusion of league play, an All Star Team was selected. Lo and behold, I was named to the Lewis County All-Stars. It was fun to play on a team where all the players were very good at every position. Once again, I was the lead-off batter and played Left Field on the Team.

The Lewis County All-Stars were all terrific guys! We really had a couple of dynamite pitchers. Our first game in the Washington State Babe Ruth Tournament in Kirkland was with a team from West Seattle that was picked by the local paper to win first place. In fact, we were paired because our team was given little chance to compete with the boys from the big city. Ron Johnson, a curve ball pitcher from Centralia, threw a three-hitter. On that day, we hit the baseball like there was no tomorrow to win the game 10 to 1. The big-city boys cried like babies because they weren't supposed to lose. The local paper the next day said the country kids had shocked the crowd. Boy, were we proud! I had three hits out of four at bats, stole two bases, and scored twice.

The next night, unfortunately, we met a southpaw who threw "white smoke" which was impossible to see let alone hit. We lost three to zip. Our trip to the Babe Ruth World Series back East was over. "Wait till next year," the other guys said. But for me that won't happen.

Next year by Babe Ruth League regulations, I will be too old to play. Lucky for me, Rock Hill High School and all its mysteries, opportunities, and challenges will begin this Fall.

WON'T THAT BE SOMETHING!!!

Rock Hill

June 1, 1953

Dear God,

Thank you for my life. Thank you for Dad and Mom. Thank you for my brothers and sisters. Thank you for giving me this beautiful country in which I live. Thank you for our US Government and our Leaders. Thank you for the Rock Hill School System, its Teachers and Administrators. Thank you for my Classmates who shall always be in my heart and mind. Thank you for letting me graduate from the eighth grade with excellent grades and on time. Thank you for allowing me to know that YOU have given me Free Will to make decisions in my life. I pray that YOU will always give me the Wisdom to know what is right for my life. Please always provide Guidance when I must lead others. Please bless me with Love in my life from friends and relatives and allow me to Love them with equal passion. Please someday in the future allow me to find that special woman, my own beautiful Miss Charlotte Heart, who will share my life with intelligence, courage and a zest for challenge and opportunity.

Please grant that I shall always believe in my abilities to compete with others on the Athletic Field, in the Classroom and Life in general. When the road is hard and long, when the task is demanding, when the game is in doubt — please grant me your power to persevere. Through the Power of Prayer, may I always have the means to hear YOUR Voice of Guidance and Inspiration. May YOU always reside in me to create a Positive Mental Attitude. **May I strive to be a better person today than I was yesterday and a better person tomorrow than I am today.**

Amen,
Jim

My Father "Jupe" and his big Husky dog Juneau --
On the Job in Southeast Alaska

*The First Load of Logs. Spring 1947 Uncle Alvin on the Left.
Uncle Sandy in the Center. Dad sitting on the Right Side.
This Truck was a US Army World War II Surplus International.
Called a "Cornbinder" by the Logger*

Still Seized -- Owner Sought

SHERIFF EARL HILTON of Lewis County examines a still, reminiscent of the prohibition era, that was found in a house near Doty, along Ocean Beach Highway. No one was home so the officers smashed the 100-gallon still and started a hunt its owner. The "kettle" is supported by an arrangement of bricks.

—(Associated Press)

This special "Christmas Card" was sent to me by my Uncle Alvin from the South Pacific During World War II.

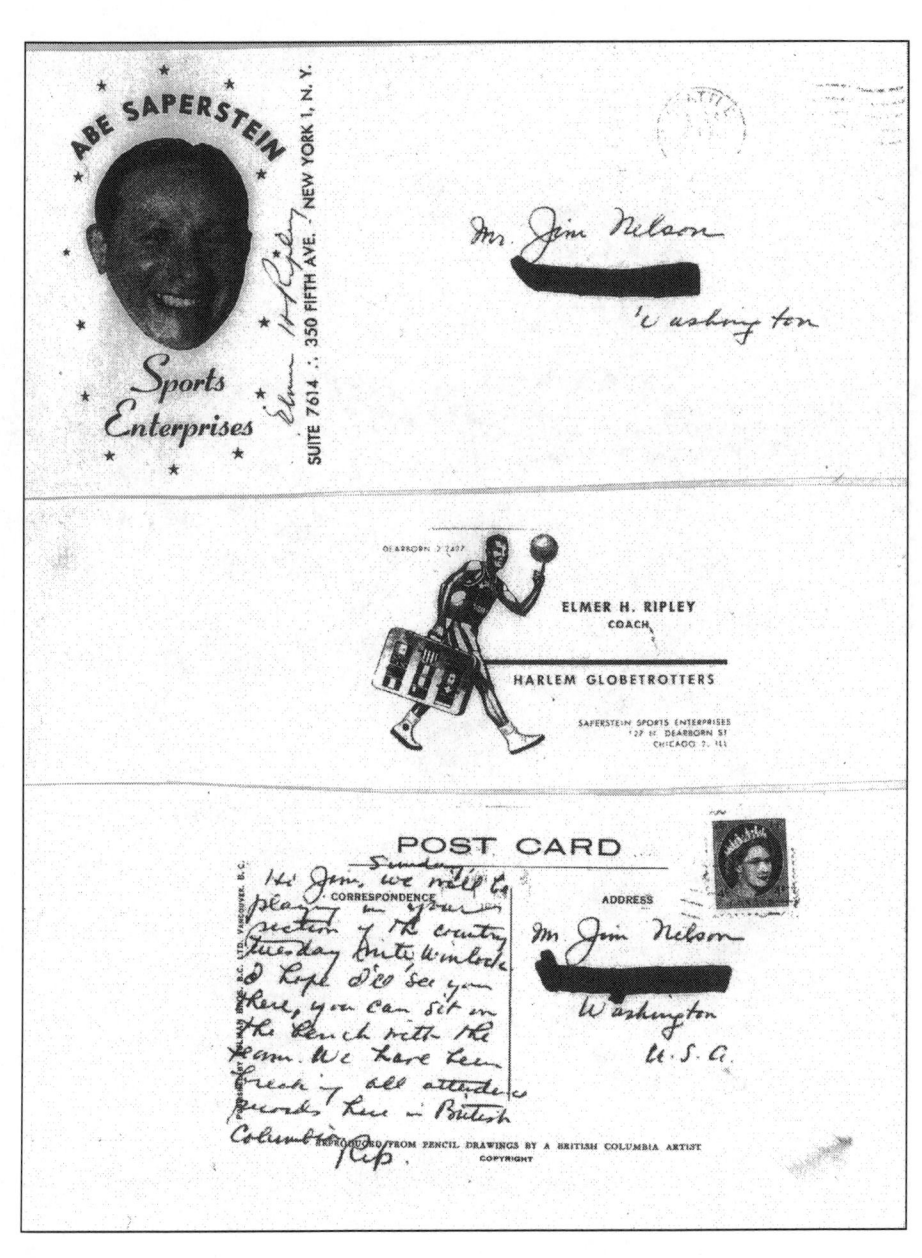

A Card to me from: "The Harlem Globetrotters."

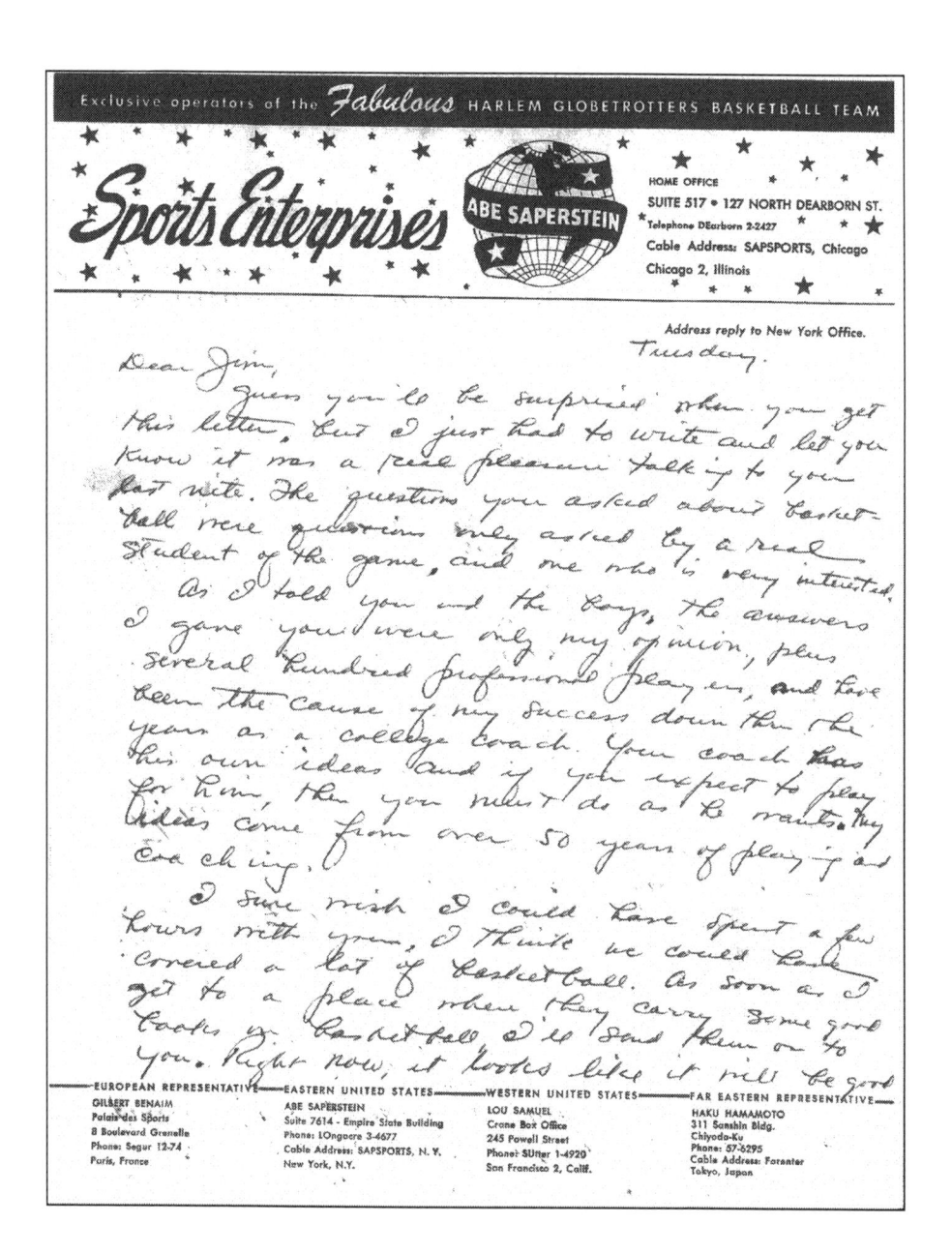

Exclusive operators of the *Fabulous* HARLEM GLOBETROTTERS BASKETBALL TEAM

Sports Enterprises

ABE SAPERSTEIN

HOME OFFICE
SUITE 517 • 127 NORTH DEARBORN ST.
Telephone DEarborn 2-2427
Cable Address: SAPSPORTS, Chicago
Chicago 2, Illinois

Address reply to New York Office.

Tuesday.

Dear Jim,

Guess you'll be surprised when you get this letter, but I just had to write and let you know it was a real pleasure talking to you last nite. The questions you asked about basketball were questions only asked by a real student of the game, and one who is very interested.

As I told you and the boys, the answers I gave you were only my opinion, plus several hundred professional players, and have been the cause of my success down thru the years as a college coach. Your coach has his own ideas and if you expect to play for him, then you must do as he wants. My ideas come from over 50 years of playing and coaching.

I sure wish I could have spent a few hours with you, I think we could have covered a lot of basketball. As soon as I get to a place where they carry some good books on basketball, I'll send them on to you. Right now, it looks like it will be good

---

EUROPEAN REPRESENTATIVE
GILBERT BENAIM
Palais des Sports
8 Boulevard Grenelle
Phone: Segur 12-74
Paris, France

EASTERN UNITED STATES
ABE SAPERSTEIN
Suite 7614 - Empire State Building
Phone: LOngacre 3-4677
Cable Address: SAPSPORTS, N. Y.
New York, N.Y.

WESTERN UNITED STATES
LOU SAMUEL
Crane Box Office
245 Powell Street
Phone: SUtter 1-4920
San Francisco 2, Calif.

FAR EASTERN REPRESENTATIVE
HAKU HAMAMOTO
311 Sanshin Bldg.
Chiyoda-Ku
Phone: 57-5295
Cable Address: Foranter
Tokyo, Japan

old N.Y. City, there one can get any thing.
Our schedule for the next week is as follows:
Tues 11 – Snohomish, Wash.
Wed 12 – Tacoma, "
Thu 13 – Everett "
Fri 14 – Bremerton "
Sat 15 – Burlington "
Sun 16 – Seattle "

May be one of those places is close to Mossy Rock, I couldn't locate it on the map, so I can't tell. You'd be welcome to visit with me and stay a couple of days. Then we really could talk basketball.

Time for me to start getting ready for our trip to Snohomish, so I'll close, again telling you what a real pleasure it was talking to a wonderful person like Jim Nelson, a real American Boy. Take care of yourself and let's hope we might meet again, some where along the way. Best and good luck, I'm going to be your pal so I'll sign,

Your Pal

Rip

The enclosed card is where you can write me, if you want.

A letter to me from: Coach Elmer H. Ripley of the "Harlem Globetrotters."

200

Elmer H. Ripley

Enshrined 1973
Staten Island, NY
July 21, 1891 - April 29, 1982

Biography

It's fitting that player and coach Elmer Ripley was born the same year that basketball was invented -- his love affair with the game lasted his entire life. After graduating from Curtis High School in Staten Island, NY, Ripley began a 20-year pro career with various teams, including Brooklyn, Washington, Cleveland, Fort Wayne, and most notably, the Original Celtics. While he was still a player, Elmer began his 26-year college-coaching career at Wagner College. He recorded great success at Georgetown, Yale, Columbia, Notre Dame, John Carroll, West Point, and Regis. A tireless leader, Ripley was constantly looking for new ways to promote basketball. Whether it was conducting clinics for players and coaches, touring with the Globetrotters, assisting the Israeli Olympic team, or coaching the Canadian Olympic team, "Rip" effectively communicated his passion and knowledge of basketball to fans across the globe. Ripley's enthusiasm for the game kept him on the bench until he was 82, just eight years before his death.

Career Highlights

- NCAA Tournament with Georgetown, 1941, 1943
- Eastern Championship with Georgetown, 1943
- Israeli Olympic team coach, 1956
- Canadian Olympic team coach, 1960

> "Sometimes the dreams of a young boy DO come True !"
>
> James A. Nelson

For those who love aviation and wish to support the Museum of Flight. Financial donations are always accepted.   www.museumofflight.org.

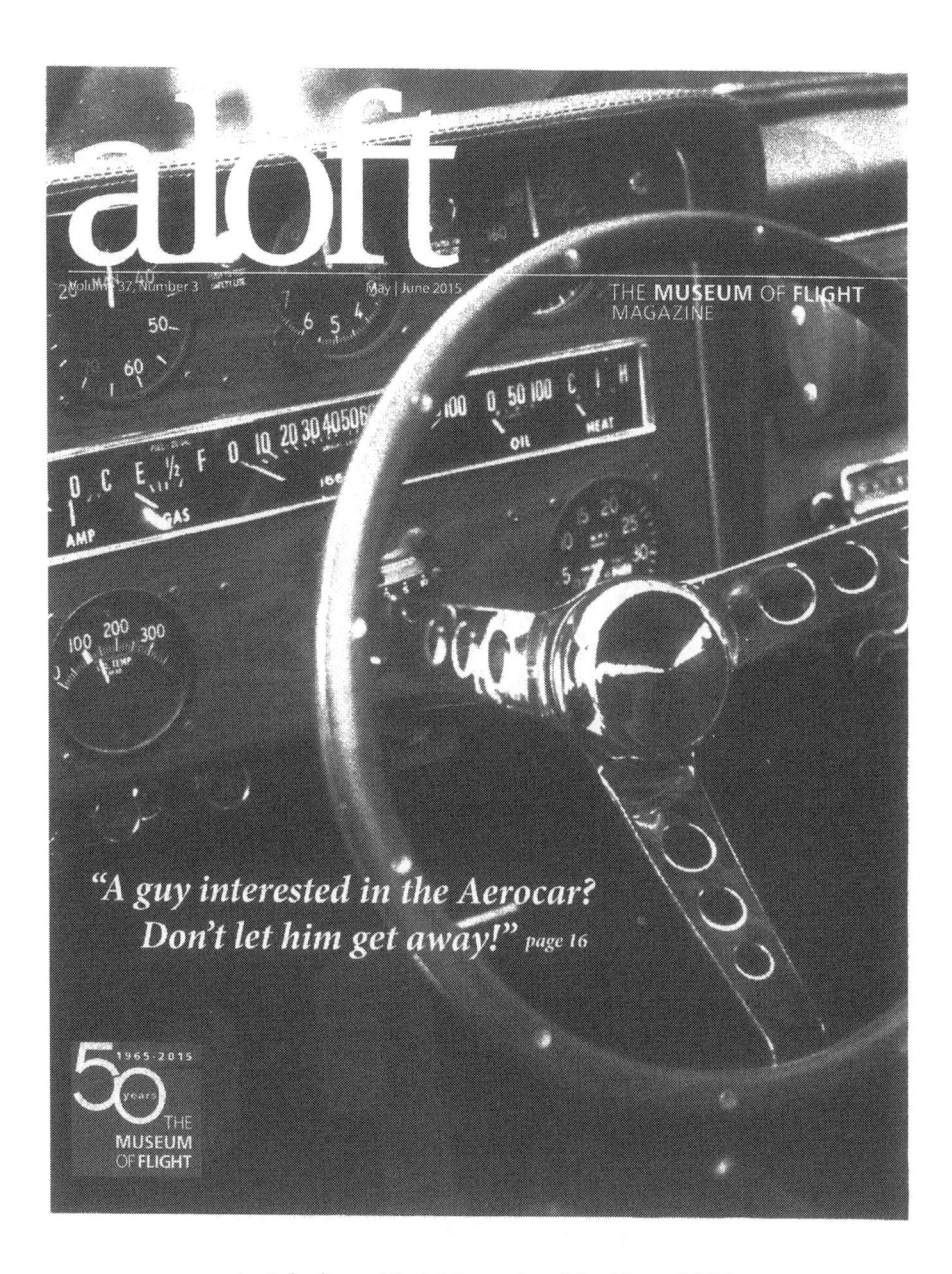

*Article from Aloft Magazine May/June 2015
is used with the permission of
Museum Of Flight, Seattle, Washington.*

203

Jim Nelson
and the great Aerocar

By: Ted Huetter,
PR Manager at The Museum of Flight

"The Aerocar was uniqueness personified."

In 1949, Rock Hill, Wash. fifth grader Jim Nelson went to an air show at nearby Longview. Formations of T-6s beat the air, a Stearman looped-the-loop, a World War II veteran with paralyzed legs did circuits in an Aircoupe with his monkey co-pilot. But for young Jim, the star was a curiosity that couldn't do much more than just takeoff and land—the Aerocar I.

The Aerocar was either a two-seat automobile that could fly or a road-able airplane depending on your point of view. It was designed and built by Longview local Moulton (Molt) Taylor, a young engineer who was passionate about the potential of a flying car. The Aerocar that captured the imagination of Jim Nelson was the first of Taylor's flying flivvers, and its maiden flight was earlier that year. It had a chubby little body reminiscent of a 1930s car without the running boards.

Taylor's dream was to make an airplane that could become a car in a matter of minutes, and visa versa. Maybe it wouldn't make airports irrelevant, but at least it would provide a simple way to drive to the airfield, fly to a distant location, then use the same vehicle to drive to your destination upon landing. Who wouldn't want something like that?

16 Aloft May | June 2015

museumofflight.org

In 1949, Rock Hill, Wash. Fifth grader Jim Nelson went to an air show at nearby Longview. Formation of T-6s beat the air, a Stearman looped-the loop, a World War II veteran with paralyzed legs did circuits in an Aircoup with his monkey co-pilot. But for young Jim, the star was a curiosity that couldn't do much more than just take off and land – the Aerocar I.

The Aerocar was either a two-seat automobile that could fly or a road-able airplane depending on your point of view. It was designed and built by Longview local Moulton (Molt) Taylor. A young engineer who was passionate about the potential of a flying car. The Aerocar that captured the imagination of Jim Nelson was the first of Taylor's flying flivvers, and its maiden flight was earlier that year. It had a chubby little body reminiscent of a 1930s car without the running boards.

Taylor's dream was to make an airplane that could become a car in a matter of minutes, and visa versa. Maybe it wouldn't make airports irrelevant, but at least it would provide a simple way to drive to the airfield, fly to a distant location, then use the same vehicle to drive to your destination upon landing. Who wouldn't want something like that?

The Aerocar worked, and Taylor tirelessly tinkered with the design throughout the fifties and early sixties. Only a few were made and one achieved some notoriety in 1961 when actor/aviator Bob Cummings flew one during his popular sit-com at the time.

In 1966 Taylor unleashed the Aerocar III. With curvy and body it was almost sporty and downright cute. Ford is said to have shown interest in manufacturing it, but without weighty bumpers it didn't meet the new federal safety regulations and the Mustang maker backed out of the deal. Others said that the Feds nixed it because there were already too many drunk drivers on the road and shuddered to think of a future with the same types of people taking to the skies as well. It is also rumored Taylor was given the ultimatum to either give up or produce and fly Aerocars in another country. Whatever the reason, it was the last Taylor Aerocar.

By 1966, Jim Nelson had become an accomplished pilot, and was a new salesman for Proctor and Gamble. His clients were spread out over the states of Wyoming, South Dakota and Nebraska. He thought that an Aerocar would be perfect for a traveling salesman, and when he heard of the model III for sale by a Cessna dealer in Springfield, Oregon, he made a deal over the phone and traded it for his Cessna 190 plus $2000 cash. This is the same Aerocar now displayed in The Museum of Flight. Jim recently came to visit her from his home in Bellevue, Wash.

⌘ ⌘ ⌘

"It really was not easy to set up and make the transition from car to plane...maybe about 30-40 minutes each time."

The Aerocar worked, and Taylor tirelessly tinkered with the design throughout the fifties and early sixties. Only a few were made, and one achieved some notoriety in 1961 when actor/aviator Bob Cummings flew one during his popular sitcom at the time.

In 1966 Taylor unleashed the Aerocar III. With a curvy red body it was almost sporty and downright cute. Ford is said to have shown interest in manufacturing it, but without weighty bumpers it didn't meet the new federal safety regulations and the Mustang maker backed out of the deal. Others said that the Feds nixed it because there were already too many drunk drivers on the road and shuddered to think of a future with the same types of people taking to the skies as well. It is also rumored Taylor was given an ultimatum to either give up or produce and fly Aerocars in another country. Whatever the reason, it was the last Taylor Aerocar.

By 1966, Jim Nelson had become an accomplished pilot, and was a new salesman for Proctor and Gamble. His clients were spread out over the states of Wyoming, South Dakota and Nebraska. He thought that an Aerocar would be perfect for a traveling salesman, and when he heard of the model III for sale by a Cessna dealer in Springfield, Oregon, he made a deal over the phone to trade it for his Cessna 190 plus $2000 cash. This is the same Aerocar now displayed in The Museum of Flight. Jim recently came to visit her from his home in Bellevue, Wash.

AS SEEN ON THE BOB CUMMINGS TV SHOW

AEROCAR
the flying Automobile

Above: The Taylor Aerocar takes to the road. (The Molt Taylor Collection/The Museum of Flight) - An image from "A Drive in the Clouds: The Story of the Aerocar." Bob Cummings was a strong supporter of the Aerocar. (The Molt Taylor Collection/The Museum of Flight)

Opposite Page: Jim Nelson views the Aerocar he once owned. (Ted Huetter) - The Taylor Aerocar in flight. (The Molt Taylor Collection/The Museum of Flight)

Previous picture from p. 204. Jim Nelson views the Aerocar he once owned. (Ted Huetter) .. The Taylor Aerocar in flight. (The Molt Taylor Collection/The Museum of Flight.)

Previous picture from p. 207. The Taylor Aerocar takes to the road (The Mold Taylor Collection. The Museum of Flight – An image from "A Drive in the Clouds. The story of the Aerocar." Bob Cummings was a strong supporter of the Aerocar. "The Molt Taylor Collection. The Museum of Flight)

BUDDY NELSON'S HANGAR is as big as man's imagination. There are no locks on the doors and the only membership requirements are Curiosity, Faith, Desire and Determination.

*Jim and Yokie – a Great Pyrenees, rescued by
Jim in the state of Wyoming.
Yokie is now waiting for Jim at "Rainbow Bridge"*

Made in the USA
Columbia, SC
03 June 2024